Upside Downside

UPSIDE DOWNSIDE

How to take the sting out of business risk

Jonathan Andrews

Hutchinson Business

London   Melbourne   Auckland   Johannesburg

Copyright © Jonathan Andrews, 1987

First published in 1987 by Hutchinson Business
An imprint of Century Hutchinson Ltd
62–65 Chandos Place, London WC2N 4NW

Century Hutchinson Australia (Pty) Ltd
PO Box 496, 16–22 Church Street, Hawthorn,
Victoria 3122, Australia

Century Hutchinson New Zealand Ltd
PO Box 40–086, 32–34 View Road, Glenfield,
Auckland 10, New Zealand

Century Hutchinson South Africa (Pty) Ltd
PO Box 337, Bergvlei 2012, South Africa

Set in Baskerville 11 on 12pt
by Input Typesetting Ltd, London

Printed and bound in Great Britain by
Mackays of Chatham Ltd, Kent

British Library Cataloguing in Publication Data

Andrews, Jonathan
  Upside downside: how to take the sting
  out of business risk.
  1. Risk management
  I. Title
  658.4'03   HD61

ISBN 0–09–172280–2

Contents

Acknowledgements

I am indebted to Mario de Pace and Richard Scambler for their expert assistance on the subjects of Computer Risks and the Key Recruit Risks respectively.

I am also grateful to Lesley Smith for lots of hard work in typing this book, reading my appalling writing and pointing out various ways to improve the text.

Introduction

This is a book about management in an environment of risk — not a book on 'Risk Management', a term which has unfortunately become synonymous with arranging insurance cover — unfortunately because identifying risk and knowing how to deal with it are fundamental to the management of a business. The action which is required of managers goes far beyond insuring against losses — important though that is.

This book is written on the basis of a number of beliefs. The first is that all businesses at all times are subject to a variety of internal and external threats which place them at risk. The external threats are largely beyond the control of individual businesses and, unless precautions such as contingency plans are taken, the business can find itself suddenly and sometimes devastatingly in deep trouble.

These external threats include:

- War or civil strife disrupting trade and destroying markets
- Competitors' actions which, for example, may make a vital product obsolete
- Movements in exchange rates
- Changes in taxation
- Changes in laws or regulations
- Strikes

- Bankruptcy of a major customer
- Changes in public taste
- Natural disasters
- Changes in the price of essential supplies

Some of these events can, of course, offer an opportunity or an advantage but in the main they represent risk. The experiences of Powell Duffryn illustrate the capricious nature of the external influences and the problems which can result.

For the financial year ending March 1986, Powell Duffryn reported profits virtually unchanged from the previous year at £28.5 million. Beneath this figure are some dramatic 'swings and roundabouts' as the company responded to a variety of external influences. These included:

- Shipping profits doubled — as a result of the end of the coal miners' strike in the UK which allowed the restocking of power stations supplied by sea. (A one-off benefit).
- A decline in engineering profits caused by weak agricultural markets (*e.g.* in the USA) which no longer required the deep-well pumps the company produced.
- Fuel distribution profits down as a result of problems in the French market, despite a cold winter which raised the demand in the UK.
- Bulk liquid storage earnings down as a result of weak currencies in Spain, Australia and South Africa.

If the external threats to a business are difficult to foresee, the internal threats can also be well hidden. They include poor production planning, lack of proper financial controls, complacency in the management team, a demotivated middle-management or simply a reluctance to change in the face of a problem or an opportunity. The fact that internal threats tend to be less obvious than external ones does not mean that they are any less important to the business. Nor does it mean that they cannot be identified and dealt with.

The second belief underlying this book is that risk is inevitable: any search for a risk-free business activity is a waste of time. While risk can be reduced it can never be entirely eliminated.

Thirdly, there are stages in every business and technological development when risk looms large as a discouragement to progress. The Chernobyl disaster is a situation in which the level of emotion surrounding the development and use of nuclear power has been raised to significant heights. However, businessmen (and politicians) must put obstacles such as this in the perspective of the history of technological development. For example the supply of domestic gas is relatively unemotive, yet gas is explosive and poisonous and is piped into millions of homes. It is also stored in huge containers in areas of dense population. These are reasons for *not* having a gas industry but no one is suggesting it should be dismantled.

In a company any number of reasons for not doing something can be found. The following may be familiar:

- The customers may not like it.
- It is not in the budget.
- The shareholders may not like it.
- The unions will object.
- Prices might go up (or down).
- Training will be a problem.
- We'll never get the financial backing.
- There could be a power strike.

Whatever innovation is suggested there will always be someone who will consider it too risky. Since change is never risk-free, progress can only be made if such discouragement is overcome.

Finally, success, and its continuation, can only result from risk taking. A major function of management is to organize innovation effectively notwithstanding the risks involved.

This book therefore looks far beyond the 'insurance policy' idea of risk. It looks closely at the features a business must possess if it is to survive and progress despite the risks it faces. Personal attitudes are fundamental, as is the structure of the business and its policies. All are examined and ideas put forward for the techniques and styles necessary for success. All the case histories, whether identified or not, are taken from real life.

I do not advocate reliance on purely 'scientific' approaches to risk, and this book does not offer mathematical decision-taking techniques as a means of resolving dilemmas. The 'computer plus commonsense' approach is recommended and explained — along with some notions which will be regarded as heretical in some quarters and for which no apology is made.

An explanation is however due to women readers who will note that masculine terms are used throughout this book. This is done simply to avoid the cumbersome 'his/her, businessman/businesswoman' type of notation. In all appropriate cases personal pronouns and names should be read as including both genders.

I have made a number of recommendations in specialized areas like insurance, takeovers and legal liability. Circumstances can vary from situation to situation and even the most subtle differences can alter the position considerably. For this and other reasons it is essential that competent expert advice is obtained in such situations.

Part I

Risk — Knowing What You Are Dealing With

Chapter 1

What is risk?

Risk, like beauty, lies in the eye of the beholder. It is difficult, but particularly important, for us to define it. The businessman, whether he likes it or not, is faced with risk in everything he does — the entrepreneur is by definition a risk taker — and only if the businessman knows with what he is dealing will he be able to minimize his vulnerability.

Dictionary definitions provide little help, offering, as they do, such words as 'hazard', 'bad result', 'danger', 'chance'. Such definitions are too simple to cover the more complex matter of risk in business, where the degree of personal confidence of the risk taker is important. A situation which one manager would regard as highly risky may be regarded by another as worth a try. These widely varying views of risk can be based on differing earlier experiences or the extent to which information is available.

To complicate matters further, the damage which might result from the failure of a project may also influence the entrepreneur's view of the risk. Someone betting 25p on a football pool faces a very high chance of failure, but little likely damage. At a nuclear power station, however, there is little chance of failure but every reason to fear its consequences. So, perhaps the first conclusion that can be drawn is that a definition of risk must take into account the cost of failure.

The football pools are normally regarded as gambling — not risk-taking at all. There is a difference between the two which the businessman must be able to identify. This can best be done by gathering information and analyzing it before taking an action — as opposed to merely making an impetuous leap.

Jacob Rothschild is quoted by Jeffrey Robinson in his book *The Risk Takers* as saying that gambling and risk taking are *totally* different. 'Gambling means that you can lose everything you have staked in a short period of time and the chances of your losing everything you've staked are quite high.' Rothschild avoids gambling by putting his money on 'quality' opportunities after 'homework' has been done to assess the risks. For example, when talking about investment risks he stresses the importance of evaluating the assets and the quality of the management of the company concerned. Rothschild regards such evaluations as integral to assessing risks. This is very different from gambling.

A usable definition of risk must therefore also take account of the information available.

Taking the two factors of damage and knowledge into account the following definition emerges:-

Risk is the likelihood of significant damage resulting from pursuing a particular course of action, after careful consideration of all the ascertainable and relevant information.

At first glance this definition appears to lack a vital ingredient, namely the chance of success or failure *as well as* the chance of significant damage. However, if the action is carefully considered then the likelihood of failure will be assessed. Ways and means to reduce that likelihood will be reduced to an acceptable level. What constitutes an acceptable level is, to a great extent, influenced by the personality, experience, training and perception of the risk-taker concerned. This topic will be discussed later, where we will see how much the acceptable level varies from person to person.

How can this definition help a businessman faced with choices of action? The answer is twofold:

- First, the definition points to the necessity of assessing the chance of failure — and of finding ways to reduce the probability.
- Secondly, by stressing damage as the main criterion, the definition points to taking steps to reduce the level of damage should failure occur.

This advice sounds obvious: most business people will say that they take these precautions as a matter of routine. The sad fact is that many of them don't, for a variety of reasons, which can include:

- Time pressure — 'The MD is screaming for action.'
- Conceit — 'I have a nose for these things.'
- Complacency — 'It worked well last year.'
- Lack of responsibility — 'It's not my money.'
- Ambition — 'If this comes off it will guarantee me a place on the board.'

Conversely, a business can ossify as a result of excessive caution. Prolonged and ever more detailed analyses can delay projects indefinitely. The professional businessman will recognize that:

- Some degree of risk is inevitable.
- Doing nothing can be as dangerous as taking impetuous action.
- There is always a convincing argument to be found for further consideration of the available facts. Setting up a working party to consider the matter further, employing the services of an expert, re-checking all the figures and postponing the project until after the holidays are all examples.

The trick is to obtain the right balance between hasty action and a futile search for absolute security and certainty — neither of which exist.

The likelihood of failure

Every business must make decisions or go under as a result of change. The businessman has a choice between making these decisions in a haphazard fashion or making them on a planned basis within a long-term strategy. Decisions may be made either by the 'highly scientific' approach to decision making on the one hand, or by the 'educated guesswork' method on the other — or even some combination of both.

Throughout the 1970s, business schools and management gurus produced a range of scientific, largely mathematical, methods for decision taking. Such techniques as 'decision tree analysis' and 'exponential forecasting' were put forward as answers to the businessman's problem of uncertainty. These techniques have the merit of drawing attention to the usefulness of trying to create some sort of rational picture from such facts, figures and opinions as may be available. Mathematical techniques, however, can be taken to absurd lengths, and still are in some businesses. A series of guesstimates is made, e.g. on market size, price levels or raw material costs, and put into a formula. The formula is evaluated and the results produced to two decimal places. The board of directors will then solemnly make a decision on what appear to be figures brought down from Mount Olympus. The process has turned an accumulation of rough estimates into apparently certain figures. Even if, say, five out of six of the original figures had been exactly right, the error in the sixth figure might have resulted in a very misleading answer.

The more numerate businessman uses the mathematical techniques to provide a *range* of possible outcomes to the project including a 'worst' scenario, a 'best' scenario and a number of intermediates. He then applies his judgment.

In many cases where a substantial decision is needed important figures are missing. These are normally related to future events. In such cases past records are used to forecast future situations. Great care is needed in extrapolating the figures but in some situations accurate forecasts can be made. Classic examples can be found in the insurance industry.

Motor insurers have an enormous amount of information available to them, including:

6

- The number of types of vehicles in use
- The number of accidents by:
      age of driver
      occupation of driver
      type of vehicle
      age of vehicle
      cause of accident
      geographical location
- Details of policy holders and the vehicles they are using

Given all this information, along with crime statistics, it should be possible for insurance companies to forecast future losses with a high degree of accuracy, and to set premiums accordingly. In reality they often fail to do so, and regularly complain about losses as a preliminary to raising premiums. For example, September 1986 saw rises of 10% in insurance costs for British motorists (well above the rate of inflation) following an announcement by the Association of British Insurers that companies were making record losses. One company raised its premium levels by 9% in January 1986 and was planning a further 10% before the year was out. This is a clear example of ample statistical evidence failing to result in a reliable forecast — unless of course the motor insurers ignore the data, make no forecast and merely put the price up whenever losses are made!

The likelihood of failure is a vital adjunct to the definition of risk and so also is the method used for assessing it. The alternative methods and some practical ideas are discussed later. The 'carefully considered' action which includes a work-manlike assessment of the likelihood of failure (or to put it more positively, the likelihood of success) is the factor which distinguishes 'creative risk taking' from gambling.

Reward and penalty

The penalty of losing a small stake on a football pool is at one end of the risk spectrum. At the other there are some dramatically costly examples of penalties for losing.

The definition of risk provided on page 4 refers to significant damage but *not* to an attractive reward if the action is successful. Clearly, a reward in the form of profit must be sought but the possibility of a huge reward must not allow the businessman to be blinded to the possibility of failure and the degree of consequent damage. Whatever the size of the likely reward for success the *professional* businessman will choose his course of action after 'careful consideration' — anything less is gambling.

Individual attitudes to risk

Regardless of the information available and the magnitude of the potential rewards or penalties, managers, being human, will allow their emotions to play a large part in deciding whether to opt for an action or not. The influence of personal emotions will vary from case to case, but some years ago a lecturer from Columbia University told a group of business people that his research showed that there was no such thing as a purely objective decision. Every decision, he believed, was influenced by emotion and many were dominated by it. This may seem a harsh judgement on all of us in business who would prefer to believe that we base our business activities on facts, figures and logic. The truth is that the man from Columbia University is right, as the following real-life cases illustrate:

Paddy, administration director of a finance company, was two years from retirement and beginning to 'wind down'.
   A well-researched proposal was put to the board which, if successful, would substantially reduce costs and improve company efficiency. About one third of the board were strongly in favour of the proposal and about one third (led by Paddy) were equally strongly opposed. The remaining directors, who were involved in the more commercial, sales-orientated side of the business, had no strong feelings either way — generally they regarded administration as a subject that concerned their colleagues and not themselves.
   Much lobbying went on prior to formal discussions of the proposal. Paddy did all he could to discredit the idea. Skilful use was made of emotive expressions such as:

'It has always worked well so why change it?'
'Staff morale is pretty low and this will only make things worse.'
'What proof is there that the benefits listed in the proposals are achievable?'

Gradually the seeds of doubt were sown. In due course the idea was rejected although not one tangible reason was produced to oppose the proposals. The whole discussion remained at the 'I'm not too happy with this idea old boy' level.

Some time later, after he had retired, Paddy commented to a former colleague how glad he was that the idea had been rejected since, if it had not, he would have had an unattractively busy last two years with responsibilities he was anxious to avoid! It seems that all of Paddy's objections to the scheme were founded on his own (unspoken) wish not to be bothered.

In another example, a project was given the go-ahead and responsibility placed with Michael, the head of management services. Michael was more than a little worried about his new task: he knew that while success would benefit his career, failure would be very damaging. Part of the project involved moving a number of functions to an out-of-town location and the plan provided for recruitment and training of new staff there. Existing staff were to be offered generous redundancy terms. Michael, lacking the confidence to depend entirely on the new recruits, offered, on his own initiative, substantial financial benefits to the existing staff to move temporarily to the new location.

The result was that the project budget was significantly overspent, a number of jobs had, for a time, two incumbents and the people who had moved were able to claim compensation *and* their redundancy pay. Additional costs were incurred for hotel bills, rail fares and even wages for gardeners to look after neglected gardens! All of this additional cost resulted from Michael's lack of confidence. An objective, independent assessment revealed that Michael's actions were entirely unnecessary.

A small company was offered an opportunity to broaden its activities into a potentially very profitable new field. The company had been heavily dependent on one source of income, so the diversification made sense. No threat was posed to the existing business and no significant capital would be at risk. The whole scheme seemed ideal — particularly for the long-term health of the business. However, to the surprise of the proposers the scheme was turned down and when they reiterated the long-term advantages one of the directors replied, 'I am sure that's true but the business as it is will see me out.' This was the attitude of the majority of the board who saw no point in doing something from which future generations would benefit.

Such reactions are only too familiar to consultants. They encounter obstacles such as the 'not invented here' and the 'We've always done it this way' syndrome. Most of these examples concern an unwillingness to act in a positive way — based on an emotional argument. The opposite can be found where action *is* taken but for reasons of personal pique, ego and blind ambition.

The head of a large industrial concern insisted that his company acquire an expensive and wholly unsuitable computer system simply because he felt that his personal reputation demanded it. Another prominent leader was prepared to take a particular action knowing it would put the organization at risk solely in order to gain personal publicity. In fact it worked — the person concerned ended up in an honours list! The organization did indeed suffer but only the insiders knew about it and they have been too frightened to say anything.

Attempts have been made to measure these emotional motivators in what is known as 'risk aversion'. This is probably of only academic interest in that aversion to risk cannot be measured in tangible units. The psychologist can work out *theoretical* tables showing, for any one individual, his willingness or otherwise to accept a risk depending on a combination of what is at stake and what the reward for success may be.

The tables might show that if a businessman has £10,000

capital he will not risk it for a potential reward of £10 but may risk it for a potential reward of £10 million. Alternatively, he may have a low risk aversion to putting up only £100 of his capital for the prospect of gaining £200.

The last case satisfies the criterion of avoiding significant damage (*i.e.* the £10,000 capital is still largely intact even if the project fails) while going for the £10 million opportunity is a response to greed and probably a gamble. The notion of risk aversion is convenient but not a practical technique in a world where many factors, in addition to stake and reward, will influence the decision taking process and the individual's perception of risk.

Risk and social pressures

Some of the social pressures — status and ambition — have already been mentioned as factors influencing attitudes to risk taking. There are others which the businessman should be aware of. They include:

- Doing a favour for an 'old school chum'. It is not unknown for someone to put money into a venture or encourage others to do so for sentimental reasons or because of a sense of loyalty to another individual.
- Making (or not making) an investment to keep a third party happy.

Politicians will put money (other people's money) into ventures, without consideration of the facts and for purely social reasons — one of the most obvious in post-war years being the East African groundnut scheme. Millions of pounds were wasted in East Africa when tons of groundnuts were rotting in West Africa for lack of a means to move them to the coast.

The businessman cannot afford such errors and must, as far as possible, objectively identify the risk in any venture, measure it in some way and take steps to minimize it. The remainder of this book will be concerned with these activities.

Summary

1.   Each individual's perception of risk varies as does his view of the risk present in any given business situation. It is important therefore for entrepreneurs to use a definition of risk to focus attention on the factors which can be damaging and those which can be helpful. Doing this will improve the chances of taking an objective decision.

2.   The professional businessman will make a distinction between gambling and risk taking, recognize the former and avoid it.

3.   Some degree of risk is inevitable in every commercial situation. A strategic approach is necessary, including policy decisions as to how risk will be evaluated.

4.   There are too many failures, even when ample statistical evidence is available, to place reliance on scientific analysis. Something more is needed to deal adequately with risk.

5.   The size of the potential reward for success and emotional thinking can be causes of bad decision taking. Ways must be found to limit irrational actions without turning the process into a purely mathematical activity, which can be equally misleading.

Chapter 2

Types of risk

Small risks, ranging from giving the cleaning contract to a different supplier to replacing the typewriters with a word processor are common in every business. They are so marginal in terms of damage if something goes wrong as to be normally unrecognized as real risks at all. The things that are recognized as risks are the major changes which cost time and money to create and which, if they fail, will have painful if not fatal results. There is, in addition, another risk which only too frequently goes unrecognized — doing nothing in a changing world. Someone at sometime no doubt made a good living from manufacturing saddles for horses. Hopefully he switched to steering wheels, tyres or sparking plugs before it was too late. Sticking with the saddles must have been a risk after a certain point in the development of other forms of transport and delaying the change too long would have killed the business.

A third category of risk is presented by the wholly unexpected external influence which can destroy the environment of the business virtually overnight. This happened to some farmers following the Chernobyl nuclear disaster, and to the abattoirs in Cumbria which were bankrupted by a government ban on slaughtering lambs. The prudent businessman will guard against this third category by ensuring that he does not have all his eggs in one basket. He will avoid concentrating his sales in volatile export markets. There are some unhappy companies who have done business in unstable regimes still waiting to be paid for goods delivered months or years ago.

The two major categories of risk

All risks fall within one or other of two categories. These are:

- Pure risks
- Entrepreneurial risks (also termed speculative risks)

Pure risks are those which arise from natural causes or other events not directly related to the commercial course of action that the business is following. Examples of pure risks include fire, earthquakes, wars, strikes, death of key staff or political action, *e.g.* tax increases.

Entrepreneurial risks arise as a result of actions taken by the business — and in some cases the actions of other, competitor, businesses. The entrepreneurial risk includes factors within the control of the business, like product design, advertising and publicity, market research and level of funding. In other words the business can influence the degree of risk. Entrepreneurial risks cannot normally be guarded against by insurance — often a hallmark of the pure risk. They can however be guarded against by paying care and attention to the need, or otherwise, for innovation, the internal and external environment which will affect the business, and all the factors which will have an influence on levels of success.

While pure risks can be important if they are not adequately recognized, they can normally be covered by insurance and are discussed in this context in a later chapter. Their nature is normally better understood than that of the entrepreneurial risk so let us, at this stage, look at some specific examples of the entrepreneurial risk.

Some examples of entrepreneurial risks

The new product or service

This is perhaps the most common of all innovative risks. Tompkins Traps Ltd had been making and selling the Mouse Mangler trap for many years, but felt that sales would be enhanced by introducing a new model.

The research and development team worked hard to design the new mousetrap and came up with a high-tech model which everyone thought would capture the imagination of the public and rapidly become the market leader. The new model was made from super high-density polypropylene (in a range of colours) and was duly launched at the Pest Control Officers' Conference in Harrogate. Advertisements appeared in appropriate magazines and the sales force raced from city to city visiting all the major outlets.

Unfortunately no one wanted the new model. It was too expensive and the old wooden trap did the job well enough. To all but the management of Tompkins Traps Ltd it was obvious that the project would fail. Anyone could see that the mouse-trapping industry did not need a high-tech solution to a low-tech problem — and would not pay the inevitably high price for it. A good and well-established product already existed so the chances of success were slim indeed.

All very far-fetched? A fictional situation with no relevance to real life? Not at all! Managements *do* act like Tompkins Traps acted and great new schemes collapse under the harsh realities of the world outside the boardroom or laboratory. Such a case is that of Britain's Freeports some of which were still without a customer *two years* after being set up.

Millions of pounds were invested in the early 1980s in the confident belief that British and foreign firms would use the freeports to import goods, process them and re-export them. The attraction would be that duty would not be payable so long as the goods did not find their way on to the domestic market.

A number of reasons for failure has been put forward and one of the most convincing is that stated by Robert

15

Rothschild of Lancaster University. Rothschild is reported as saying that failure was inevitable because Britain's freeports could not compete with long-established European zones such as Hamburg or Rotterdam. In other words, a satisfactory mousetrap already existed. Other reported contributory factors were restrictive labour practices, uncertainty over taxation policy and high labour costs in relation to overseas competitors. So, not only was there doubt that the trap would catch the mouse but it was too expensive as well!

A *Financial Times* report on the freeports (August 19th, 1986) included the information that since February 1984 only two freeports had had any measurable success, one had not even begun to market itself and three were in serious trouble. In Belfast, where about half of the freeport jobs were to be found, the companies in the zone were there more as a result of the proximity of the airport than the freeport itself.

Grants in the rest of the province were so high that there was little incentive for a company to site itself within the freeport. Bristol had received 400 enquiries but no customers; there was *hope* that the government would change the taxation rules to make the zones more attractive; Prestwick was clearly under capitalized and blame was being placed on Customs and Excise for the failure of the freeport to make any impact. Only Liverpool and Southampton had shown any degree of success — both locations having long established and traditional links with importers and exporters.

This example of an innovation going wrong also illustrates the emotional and social pressures, mentioned in the previous chapter, which can influence a business decision. It has been alleged that the government undermined the freeports by choosing the wrong ones in the wrong places. The logical places, in view of Britain's increasing dependence on European trade, would have been on the east coast — Hull, Felixstowe or Aberdeen for example. Southampton did make sense but the planners also ignored Heathrow and London's docklands.

What then governed the choice? The idea of the freeports arose from a select committee report and the choice deteriorated into nothing more than a political battle. In other words, any semblance of rational business decision gave way to the politicians' desires.

There are many more examples of innovative risk going wrong — Clive Sinclair's C5 motorized car and Eddie Shah's *Today* being fresh in the memory. However, a look at a successful venture is called for, both as an example of the new product type of risk and to whet the appetite for the measures which can be taken to successfully reduce risk which are described in later chapters.

The successful venture is a company called Interlink which is one of the largest overnight parcel delivery services in Britain. Founded by Richard Gabriel — who in 1979 was a motorcycle messenger battling through the London traffic — the company now has over 100 regional depots and handles around 10,000 parcels at its sorting centre each night. Despite a very tough market with lots of competition, including the large and well established TDG and National Freight, Gabriel has succeeded. How he did it is important to all risk takers.

The success of Interlink was based on Gabriel's analysis of the market and his reaction to the results of that analysis. The main points were:

- As a first priority, Gabriel identified the weaknesses of the existing companies in the field.
- He spotted high overheads and poor cost control. He noticed, for instance, that lorries would make journeys fully loaded but return empty.
- He spotted administrative nonsenses, such as complicated tariffs which customers found difficult to understand.
- Customers wanted a low cost, efficient and dependable overnight service and were not getting it.

In other words Gabriel looked at the business from the customer's point of view and rightly concluded that costs could be cut by efficient administration which, at the same time, could include systems to ensure that the service met the standards customers were looking for.

Gabriel, convinced that he could do better than the

17

existing companies in the business, now faced a major problem — how to raise the substantial capital required to set up what had to be a nationwide network. He found the solution in franchising — not merely a means to find the money but also a means to *share the risk*. He involved, in the form of franchisees, a number of other entrepreneurs who put up money for a personal stake in the business.

The professional mistake

In the USA, particularly in California, gynaecologists and other medical specialists are giving up their work because they cannot afford, or cannot get, insurance against professional errors. Malpractice suits with enormous compensation awarded by the courts have made the risk intolerable.

In the UK, shipbroker members of the Baltic Exchange are obliged, as a condition of their membership, to have at least £100,000 cover for liabilities. Some would regard this as inadequate when the potential costs of a professional error are examined. Suppose for example that a shipbroker's client asks for a ship to be chartered to take 10,000 tons of cargo from the UK to a port in Chile. The shipbroker will seek a suitable vessel, negotiate a price and 'fix' the charter on behalf of his client. The client, satisfied with the deal arranged on his behalf, loads his cargo on board and looks forward to the profits resulting from a well planned transaction.

The broker's clerk may however have made a mistake and failed to check that the draught of the vessel was suitable for the port of destination. If the vessel was not able to dock in the port concerned then the cargo must either be taken ashore by lighter or landed at another port and sent by road or rail to its intended destination. The costs involved in such an exercise can be enormous, combined with an increased risk of loss or damage to the cargo, delays in delivery resulting in lost sales and the unavailability of the ship to pick up another cargo or commence a new charter at a pre-arranged time.

The chances are that the broker's client can successfully sue the broker for negligence and recover the losses incurred. Salt will be rubbed into the wound if it is also discovered that due to another error the clerk quoted the wrong price to the client company — an error not unknown in shipping circles. The broker may well be faced with paying the difference out of his own pocket.

Lawsuits for professional negligence have been made against firms of accountants — including some of the major names in the profession — and they too are having problems with insurance costs. Many others face the professional liability risk whenever they carry out another transaction in their chosen field.

One of the most important aspects of this type of risk is that many practitioners in the various professions are unaware of them. For example, suppose a ship manager has, as part of his contract, a duty to find crew members. Suppose also that the ship collides with another ship with the loss of both vessels. If it can later be shown that the officer on watch in the 'guilty' ship was not qualified then the manager who selected him for the job could be held liable for the disaster. Not every ship management company is aware of this risk and some have not taken precautions against it.

Likewise, leasing companies use indemnity clauses in their contracts with lessors, such that if anything goes wrong and, say, the vehicle, photocopier or whatever is faulty and kills someone, the lessee takes responsibility. Such contractual clauses might not stand up in court in view of the Unfair Contract Terms Act and the leasing company could find itself in unexpected trouble.

In summary, although professional mistakes may not at first sight appear to be entrepreneurial risks they can only result from action taken in the course of business. The entrepreneurial nature of those risks becomes more apparent when the professional firm enters a new field. A leasing company extending its activities from office equipment into small aircraft is changing the nature of the business and exposing itself to a whole new, and different, range of threats. Even the country solicitor who adds to his will, divorce and conveyancing work the task of advising a manufacturing company on product liability is making a change which has potential for trouble.

19

Mergers and takeovers

A takeover battle can be costly for winners as well as losers, as illustrated by the Dixon/Woolworth case in 1986.

While it has been estimated that the failed bid cost Dixon £14 million, Woolworth was estimated in the newspapers to have paid out £20 million, including the cost of all the advertisements appearing in the national press at the time. Woolworth management stated that the £20 million estimate was 'far too high' but at only half that amount we are talking about the equivalent of a massive amount of gross sales profit — which is one way to look at it.

The damage which may be caused is often not only financial. The increasing bitterness creeping into the public statements of the antagonists and the increasing abusiveness of the comments about their rivals does nothing for the image of those concerned. As one business executive remarked after hearing the remarks of a would-be takeover victor on television, 'Evil little devil isn't he?'

When a buyout, or agreed merger, takes place the potential for further damage emerges. At the higher levels of management there is often some cynical trade-off as ambitious executives sacrifice whole departments to preserve or improve their personal position. High-quality staff can be ditched overnight.

A cost of takeovers and mergers can be long-running disputes between the managers from the two sides, making rational business decisions difficult to achieve. The savings from rationalisation are far from certain, often as a result of the personalities involved and their opposing ambitions.

New technology

The risk in new technology is both internal and external. Internally the risk lies in adopting or not adopting a new technology and the external risk comes from the competition, which may successfully exploit it.

The watchmaking industry offers some good examples, with many established companies having a hard time when the first liquid crystal display watches appeared. Their product, of the traditional analogue type, was at risk and so also was the whole traditional Swiss watch industry. In the 1970s the volume watch market was taken over when Japan and other Far Eastern countries saturated the market with cheap electronic products. Only at the top of the quality range did the traditional manufacturers maintain dominance.

An interesting reversal of the trend has occurred in the mid-1980s with the appearance of the Swatch and, later Le Clip. These stylish analogue watches are being sold as a fashion accessory as much as time pieces — taking advantage of a society where the possession of two or more watches chosen to complement dress style is feasible.

The latest idea, and possibly another threat to the high-tech watch makers, is a watch capable of receiving radio signals and displaying messages. Just about every manufactured product is threatened by new technology and every new technology product presents a risk to its developers.

Research and development

Closely linked to the new technology risk is the R & D risk. The company sensing danger from competitors — or concluding that an opportunity exists for a new product — must decide whether to invest the necessary resources in R & D. Thousands of pounds (in some cases millions of pounds) may be required to develop a new product which may turn out to be a flop. At worst the work may be entirely unsuccessful and produce no new saleable product at all.

On the other hand, to do nothing in the face of uncertainty can also be disastrous as the successfully innovative competitor may capture the market.

There has often been anguish in a boardroom when the Sales Director demands a new or improved product, the R & D Director states how much money he will need and the Finance Director declares that the expenditure will bankrupt the company. The Sales Director will complete the circle by declaring that without the new product the company will go bust anyway.

Organizational change

Problems created by growth — in number of employees, markets and product range — can prompt a business to reorganize itself. The project is sometimes limited to moving a few people about, centralizing (or decentralizing) a service function or two and issuing a new organization chart showing who's who. Such reorganizations are likely to disappoint those who gained nothing, and to bewilder those who are struggling to sort out what their new responsibilities are.

At a more sophisticated level, organizational change can improve leadership, the business and the market. Waste can be cut, decision taking speeded up and the whole tempo of the business raised to a new level. In other words the organizational framework is updated to make it receptive to management methods which will make the business more effective.

The risk here lies in not doing the job properly or not doing it at all. A badly managed organizational change can be very destructive — not least by demotivating the people.

The cost-cutting exercise

In 1986 a report of a study covering twenty five companies was published in the USA, which drew attention to a risk which frequently goes unrecognized. This is the risk that a cost-cutting exercise may fail to make the company more competitive — it may even worsen the situation. The reasons given for failure are:

- Cost-cutting usually results in only marginal productivity improvements.
- The direct labour costs which are normally the main area of attack are rarely a large enough proportion of the total cost to provide any real opportunity.
- Attention is taken away from long-term thinking and, what is more crucial to production costs, the production system itself.
- Attention is drawn away from other factors influencing

competitiveness such as product quality, customer service and production flexibility.
- Managers are tied up dealing with low-level and short-term considerations to the detriment of strategic work.
- Cost cutting discourages innovation.
- A negative attitude (and possibly a depressing atmosphere) develops among the work force.

Such conclusions may surprise managers who have believed, and have been encouraged to believe, that cutting waste and inefficiency is the route to significantly improved competitiveness. The fact is, and there are case histories to prove it, that despite these measures *productivity* remains largely unchanged. There is perhaps a difference between cost cutting (which implies crude and arbitrary action) and cost reduction (which implies some careful thought and planning).

Summary

These then are some of the risks a business may face. There are many others, some of which are further examined in the last part of this book where readers can look for comments and suggestions in respect to particular risks which may concern them.

The selection of risks given in this chapter illustrates many of the characteristics of risk situations:

1   The risk element in an action is not always obvious.
2   The risk in a situation is often related to the end user of the product or service — simply stated, the customer may not need it, want it or like it.
3   Risk is increased by emotional reaction and failure to maintain an objective approach.
4   No matter how good the product or the company may be the human element can cause failure.
5   Risk can be increased by failure of management to act as a single-minded team.
6   Many risk situations are created by lack of technical, professional or management skills somewhere in the system.

7   Managements often ignore the realities of life and may make poor decisions as a result of not being sufficiently market-orientated. Conversely, dramatic success can be achieved and risk greatly reduced by clearly identifying customer needs.

8   Opportunities to share risk, *e.g.* by franchising and insurance must be used to the full (see Chapter 7).

9   Management is not always aware of the variety of risks facing it and ways must be found to reduce this weakness.

Part II

The Measurement of Risk

Chapter 3

Luck and judgement

The risk in a business situation depends on the correctness or otherwise of the decisions that the businessman makes regarding that situation. If, by good judgment or good luck, he makes the best decision he will at least have reduced the risk. Conversely, the wrong choice can result in damage which, in crucial cases, can be disastrous.

The dilemma of deciding which is the best course of action to take has faced people since time began. Ways and means to reduce risk have been developed over the centuries and include the establishment of trade guilds in the Middle Ages and the mutual forms of insurance which emerged in 17th century London. Even earlier recorded methods of risk reduction can be found in ancient Greece and Phoenicia where forms of insurance were practised. No doubt, in those earlier days, entrepreneurs, merchants and financiers agonized like their present-day counterparts over whether or not an investment was likely to succeed or fail. They must have debated whether or not money invested in a voyage would yield a good return — or none at all.

A major difference in say, the 18th century, compared with today, was the lack of information available to the businessman. Information on the availability and prices of goods in markets many weeks' voyage away was inevitably out of date and there was, in many ways, greater uncertainty than there is today. Voyage durations were dependent on winds rather than diesel power, and a cholera epidemic could wipe out an entire trading station months before a cargo ship arrived.

Despite the technological developments of the 20th century which have removed many of the problems facing the merchant venturer of old, uncertainty still exists. The same technology which has removed some uncertainties has, at the same time, changed the rules of the game in a number of ways and has created new uncertainties. For example it is now possible with modern communications and almost universally available technical know-how for a competitor to enter a market to compete with a successful innovation within weeks or months of the launch of the new product. In other words, there is less certainty of a lengthy clear run for a new idea.

This continuing uncertainty, which will no doubt persist, gave rise to the development of 'scientific' approaches to decision taking in the years following World War Two. Many of these scientific methods, based on mathematics, arose from operations research techniques developed for military purposes during the war. The generals needed to know, for example, the likely outcome in terms of direct hits, of the alternative ways for bombers to attack their targets. Work was done to create mathematical formulae to show which of high-level daylight raids, low-level daylight raids, low-level night attacks and so on would result in the most damage to the enemy — and at what cost in terms of lost planes and aircrew killed.

Peacetime developments of this wartime thinking led to operations research techniques, for business purposes, such as:

- Standard deviation analysis
- Probability theory
- Simulation and model building
- Linear programming
- Queuing theory
- Exponential forecasting
- Decision tree analysis

Some businessmen were, and still are, strongly attracted to these methods while others totally reject them. There is no doubt that in the 1960s and 1970s many businesses suffered from placing too much reliance on what came to be regarded as 'magic formulae' for success. Common sense was too often neglected.

An example occurred in a company producing man-made fibres. They had the problem, like most businesses, of forecasting customer demand for their product and were deeply concerned that every time that the forecast was significantly wrong, money was lost either as a result of not producing enough of a product to meet customer demand, or of producing too much. It was decided to use a mathematical forecasting technique and to employ the technique on a computer. The argument put forward was that the traditional forecasting — based on salesmen's estimates — was nothing more than a collection of guesses. By using a technique which extrapolated past sales figures, it was argued, a more reliable result would be achieved.

It so happened that sales of one of the main products in the company's range had been increasing in recent months and a particular colour (black) was more and more in demand. The computer, using a formula which placed proportionately greater weight on the more recent months, produced a forecast of rapidly rising demand for the black product.

In consequence production of the black product was increased substantially and resources switched to it from other, less favoured products. Unfortunately sales did not match the forecast and the company was left with huge stocks.

The reason for this disaster was simply that the company's products were sold to the clothing industry — an industry more than usually at the mercy of the vagaries of fashion. It should not have been too great a surprise to the company that the teenage market, hitherto dedicated to black garments, had suddenly changed its mind. By the time stocks of black material had been produced the customers would not be seen dead in it!

Was it wrong therefore to use the mathematical method? The answer is no. It was not wrong to use it to obtain an indicator of the future — the computer would have produced arithmetically correct figures and it is not unreasonable to use past results as a guide to the future. The mistake lay in not applying common sense to the answers provided by the computer and by ignoring other data from the past which showed that the life of any particular colour could be short. Had the figures been reviewed by the sales force before being applied they would almost certainly have been modified as a result.

The problem of the misleading extrapolation is well and amusingly illustrated by a report which appeared some years ago from the intelligence unit of a national newspaper. Apparently some statistics had been produced showing that the average height of women in England had increased over a period of eight years at a rate of 0.1% per year. At the same time bust sizes had increased from an average of 34" to an average of 36". Applying a standard statistical technique to these figures revealed that by the year 2071 Englishwomen would average 5' 11" in height and have a six foot bust!

Experience, except in the purely scientific world (*e.g.* engineering, design and chemical analysis) strongly suggests that the majority of business dilemmas cannot be solved by applying a textbook formula.

1   The data collected may not be reliable. Changes can, and do, occur during or following a collection period. British government methods for producing unemployment figures have changed markedly during the 1980s and are a classic example of variability in the *meaning* of a figure produced. Businesses relying on such data can be misled.
2   The unit of measurement must be specific and definite. This is not always the case, as is illustrated by the many variations on the term 'stock value'. This can include original purchase price, written down value or market value. Market value can, in some cases, be anybody's guess.
3   The data must be truly relevant to the purpose and unambiguously reflect the situation being examined. For example, it might be claimed that there has been

a 50% increase in the number of customers over the year. If however the company has gained say, twenty customers buying £1,000 worth of product each *but* has lost five customers buying £20,000 worth each, then the statement is misleading to those who think that the business is expanding.

4   Too many businessmen are blinded by science and place a value on the results of analysis which is not justified. It is rather like saying, 'It must be true, I read it in the newspaper.'

5   Mathematical methods do not allow for influences such as the prejudices of individuals, or conflicting policies or emotions.

6   The textbook formula is frequently applied in a context of rapidly changing or uncertain situations. Making allowance for the changes and uncertainties by including them in the formula, even if this is possible, normally results in such complexity and so many alternative results as to make the answer unusable.

A good illustration of this last point was found in the airline industry where, in 1986, efforts were being made to rearrange industrial insurance methods. This was prompted by ever-increasing insurance costs which in turn were prompted by record losses. 1985 was the worst year for airlines (and their insurers) since 1972. Claims exceeded a billion dollars and over 1,500 lives were lost in airline accidents in the western world.

An attempt was made, using loss records from the past, to estimate future results and to produce a business plan for the years ahead. The results of this business plan would, among other things, show the financial viability of the proposed insurance scheme. Among many variables such as reinsurance costs and the greater or lesser use of different types of aircraft, the principal uncertainty was the number of accidents which might occur. The past figures were examined and an average accident rate was taken for inclusion in the calculations. This was not, in itself, an unreasonable step to take, but the danger of placing any great reliance on the calculated outcome for future years can be gauged by a quick look at the accident figures for earlier years.

IATA have published the following figures for their member airlines —

	Fatal Accidents	
	per 100 million kilometres flown	per 100,000 aircraft [hours flown]
1980	0.15	0.09
1981	0.09	0.06
1982	0.10	0.06
1983	0.16	0.10
1984	0.08	0.05

It will be seen that the figures fluctuate considerably from year to year and since the loss of a jumbo jet along with say, 400 lives, can cost as much as $250 million (a figure of $1 billion is not beyond the bounds of possibility) then the fluctuations in accident rates can represent huge year-by-year differences in financial results. No one can even remotely guess how many major airline disasters will occur in any given future year, however many mathematical models are prepared or business plans produced on the computer. The best that can be done is to calculate the financial results of a very good year with no major accidents and a very bad year with many major accidents. (What constitutes a major accident, what the cumulative effect of minor accidents could be and what is meant by 'many' accidents also needs to be clarified.) It can then be reasonably (but not wholly) assumed for the purposes of planning that the actual results will fall between the two extremes. The *profit* result is not truly fore-castable, and from the insurer's point of view the business would be a pure gamble if it were not for reinsurance being used to spread any losses far and wide.

The danger lies in someone using the sort of figures produced in this airline example as if they were holy writ, forgetting that the whole outcome may depend on such things as storms, freak winds, metal fatigue and whether or not a pilot was 100% fit and well at a particular time.

Another example which illustrates the fallibility of fore-

32

casting — and official statistics — is the M25 motorway encircling London. The motorway was built to relieve massive congestion on roads into and around the city but within weeks of the opening of the various sections it was seen that the new road was a failure. The motorway itself, even when fully open, was grossly overcrowded and, in some places, more difficult to use than the older roads it was intended to replace. It became clear that the traffic density forecasts which resulted in a decision to build a three-lane road were hopelessly wrong and that in some sections at least a four-lane road was clearly needed. The official forecasts were for a traffic density up to 75,000 vehicles per day compared with the 115,000 vehicles per day actually appearing on the busier sections. The 1986 traffic flow was higher than official forecasts for 1996 and in one notorious section the 1986 flow of 70,000 vehicles a day compares with a forecast of 28,000 — after ten years!

The forecasting model used by the Department of Transport assumed that journeys made on the old roads would switch to the new road but did not allow for additional journeys generated simply as a result of the existence of the motorway. The model also made assumptions about oil prices being high and fuel costs discouraging traffic. It is now realized, too late, that some of the assumptions were wrong and also that building a motorway in an area of high vehicle use will of itself generate traffic.

There are then, dangers in using past figures to forecast future results and dangers in oversimplifying the problem — forgetting that in many cases the variables are many and not all of them are obvious. The problem of placing an unjustified validity on 'guesstimates' is well illustrated by the use of the technique, decision tree analysis.

Changing guesses into certainty

Decision tree analysis is used to help the businessman make a decision when faced with a number of choices. Although the technique should *not* be used as a means to reveal what is the best decision to make (but only which alternative provides the best result on the basis of the guesses made), that, in practice, is what happens. The technique works like this:

Suppose a business had a choice of making any one of three products — A, B or C — and that the profit will depend on the level of economic activity and will vary from product to product. The business must decide which of the three products to choose and to assist in reaching a conclusion a decision tree is prepared (see Figure 3.1).

The people preparing the decision tree have concluded that the chance of an upswing in the economy is 0.2 (20%), the chance of things staying much the same is 0.5 and that of a recession 0.3. They have also calculated the profit or loss which will result in the event of any of these circumstances arising for each of the products they can choose from.

If we assume that their profit calculations are accurate, *i.e.* the competition does nothing, and the degree of upswing or recession can only have one value, then on the face of it the decision tree is very helpful. At least they will know that the only chance of making a loss arises in the case of product A whilst product C offers a fairly attractive range of profit possibilities. Alternatively they might prefer to go for product A because of the high profit that an upswing would produce and take a chance that the recession will not occur. Product B offers some attractive profits in the event of an upswing or no change without (as in the case of A) a loss following a recession and this choice could be preferred.

The management of the business can make its choice providing that they do not forget that the whole thing depends on how accurately they guessed the chances of a recession or an upswing in the economy in the first place. In real life the profit figure shown on the decision tree resulting from the choice made is too often quoted as a firmly expected result. When the almost inevitably different outcome emerges shock and horror breaks out in the boardroom.

Sometimes, in addition, the calculation is taken a stage further to give what is known as an 'expected value'. This is worked out by multiplying the estimated probability by the outcome. Thus, using our example, product A would have an expected value of $(300 \times 0.2) + (160 \times 0.5) - (200 \times 0.3) = 60 + 80 - 60 = 80$.

Profit expected

Upswing 0.2	300
No change 0.5	160
Recession 0.3	−200
Upswing 0.2	220
No change 0.5	190
Recession 0.3	40
Upswing 0.2	170
No change 0.5	150
Recession 0.3	100

Product A

Product B

Product C

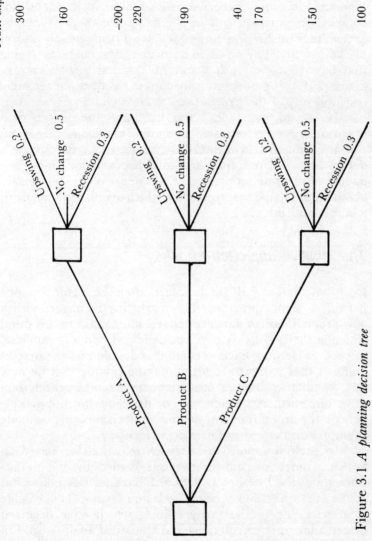

Figure 3.1 A planning decision tree

35

A similar calculation is carried out for products B and C enabling comparisons to be made between all three products. Undoubtedly the expected values are convenient for comparison purposes but how reliable are they? It can be argued that they represent nothing at all being merely a form of average and having as much value as a guide as saying that the average of 1, 2, 3 and 1,000 is 251.5. The average figure (251.5) is mathematically correct but does not remotely resemble any of the figures used to create it.

If, in addition, 1, 2, 3 and 1,000 are *estimates only* then the average is even less useful as a guide to making a decision.

In summary, whilst OR techniques can encourage a desirably structured approach to risk evaluation there is a danger of creating an illusion of certainty. What can be said about an approach to the problem which avoids mathematical analysis altogether?

The intuitive approach to risk

Decisions, large and small, must often be made by one person — under pressure. The marketing manager, with a new product launch date ever closer, must make up his mind which of the various styles of packaging, slogan and publicity to choose. He may have to come to a decision on the market segment that is most promising for the product but he may have conflicting, unclear or inadequate market research data to go on. Further research may be desirable but not acceptable on the grounds of cost or time. A decision must be made promptly on the basis of existing evidence.

In such situations the decision may well be based on hunch. Hunch or 'gut-feeling' was reviled by the purists throughout the 1960s and 1970s as a basis for risk taking but in the 1980s has slowly come back into favour. This change is in part due to the many failures which have occurred despite elaborate calculations and statistical analyses and in part due to the fact that some people can come up with the right answer without any *apparent* analysis at all. It is virtually certain, however, that behind the hunch of the experienced businessman is a process of evaluation which even the businessman himself may not be aware of. The fact is that the person acting on a hunch has used the finest computer in the world — the human brain. This tool of management has more storage capacity and greater powers to sort, compare and summarize information than any man-made machine. The brain also carries out its calculations at such speed that the 'user' is quite unable to be aware of the processes used.

In the process of developing the hunch answer the businessman is using his very personal computer to absorb the facts and opinions as stated and relate them to an accumulation of experience — much of which his conscious mind may have forgotten. This accumulated experience involves a multiplicity of small facts, warning signals and cause-and-effect memories which can be brought to bear on the problem to be solved. The fact is that this process — which cannot be written down — can be very effective.

Clearly, the hunch approach will be increasingly effective as more and more relevant information is made available. Hunch should not be confused with guessing, which is the process used when little or no information is available at all. Avoiding a sheer guess is clearly important and support of the hunch method does not provide an excuse for failing to obtain all the information that it is possible to get.

The real life situation

Whatever the pros and cons may be of using 'science' to take business decisions, the facts of real life will dominate the situation. Not only will decisions be required under circumstances of time pressure but also in circumstances of rapid change. The world outside does not stand still and rapid changes call for rapid decisions. This means that in real life the luxury of enough time to collect detailed information and analyse it exhaustively is not always available. This in turn means that the intuitive or partly intuitive action is inevitable and the risk taker needs techniques to make such action as effective as possible.

This view is strongly supported by a report published in

1986 by the Office of Technology Assessment — a United States government body. The report, entitled 'Research Funding as an Investment — Can We Measure the Return?' argues that quantitative techniques to evaluate research and development are largely a waste of time. Formalized assessments fail to take account of the personalities of the people involved and how technological results will actually be applied in marketing, production etc. The report recommends qualitative methods as simple as holding regular meetings between the executives concerned to debate the issues and reach a consensus.

Managing the decision process

The choice of method for evaluating major risk situations is a subject requiring board-level consideration. The role of top management is examined in a broader context in Chapter 8 but the style of leadership adopted is highly relevant here, since the style used will tend to limit the choice of method and because of this demands some special attention.

The most damaging style is that which positively inhibits decision taking or change by being over-centralized. This problem is illustrated below.

The chief executive of Crumbly Cake Company, Mr Nigel, inherits the business from his highly entrepreneurial father, Sir John. Mr Nigel, lacking his father's enterprise, drive and courage finds decision taking extremely worrying and difficult. He is surrounded by directors who were dominated by the ferocious personality of old Sir John and although they all believe that Mr Nigel is 'not the man his father was' they prefer to take their lead from him.

Mr Nigel follows his father's example and insists that all decisions of any consequence (and that to him means just about everything) will be taken at board level. Since he finds it difficult to make up his mind he calls for more and more detail on every topic. The company has installed a computer and, having acquired the capacity to produce miles of print-out, uses it to the full. Important company problems are buried in a morass of detail — made worse by demands for ever more information.

The crisis comes when, following falling sales of the company's main product, a competitor appears in the market with a new flavour cake mix which shows signs of becoming dominant. Mr Nigel calls for reports, analyses and opinions. The marketing director suggest a counter attack with the apricot mix which had been developed six months ago but not yet launched because Mr Nigel was not sure it would succeed.

Mr Nigel is still unsure and deferrs the decision to the next meeting in a month's time giving instructions for more customer surveys to be done and another study to be made of the competitive product. This process continues for another year and the company goes bust.

Crumbly Cakes made the following mistakes:

- The chief executive was unable to make decisions himself but would not delegate.
- The chief executive and the board were too involved in details.
- Decisions were deferred — sometimes to give the board time to obtain even more information and analyses (paralysis by analysis).
- There was too much dependence on personal influence.

Other mistakes to be avoided at top level include:

- An absence of strategy to which decisions can be related. This can result in disruptive ad hoc decisions.
- An absence of objectives
- Bureaucratic restrictions and obstacles

General Foods, one of America's Fortune 500 companies was, in the 1970s, a keen exponent of the portfolio planning technique. Use of the technique — promoted by some of the leading US management consultants — led General Foods into a potentially very damaging situation which they only just avoided. Looking back some time later Chief Executive I L Ferguson stated that concepts such as the portfolio grid and the product life cycle are very good in theory but could get you into trouble, 'if you really believe that what is theorized will actually happen.'

Summary

1 The problem of measuring risk is an old one which was tackled in post-war years by the widespread introduction of operations research techniques. These techniques have not been generally successful largely because they have been misused. Businessmen have been dazzled by computer print-outs and scientific formulae.

2 The human element in the form of hunch has considerable value and when *combined* with the mathematical approach can lead to reduced risk.

3 Decision taking within the context of a clearly defined policy/strategy has a greater chance of success.

4 Techniques for evaluation, whether mathematical or not, must be used in a context determined by management style. If this style is not right the risk is increased.

Chapter 4

Risk assessment — some practical methods

Realistic methods are needed to assess risk, *i.e.* at least to reach a conclusion as to whether or not a proposed venture is:

1 'A hell of a gamble.'
2 'A bit chancy but it could work.'
3 'A fair proposition.'
4 'A likely winner.'
5 'A near certainty.'

The methods proposed in this chapter take account of the arguments put forward in previous chapters — they avoid too much science on the one hand and too much emotional thinking and procrastination on the other. They should not in any way be regarded as foolproof and do not remove the necessity to carry out sensible research to obtain as much information as possible on the environment surrounding the problem. They do however offer a disciplined way of assessing risk when, as is normally the case, the environment is changing and the data available are either unavoidably incomplete or of uncertain accuracy.

The methods proposed will normally provide an accept-

41

able degree of accuracy. They make full use of hunch in a world where little is exact and time is often short. Before using them there is an important preliminary stage — clarifying the objective.

The 'clarity checklist'

The first essential in assessing risk is to be absolutely sure about what the objective is. Yes, this is obvious, but experience shows that debate on whether or not an action should be taken is not infrequently carried out between executives who have different versions of the ultimate objective in mind. Another purpose of the 'clarity checklist' method is to ensure that the wrong step is not taken simply as a result of sloppy thinking. Here then are the questions to be asked:

1   Have we stated the objective?
2   Is the objective stated in clear and unambiguous terms? For example, an objective which says 'increase market share in Europe' is meaningless. A tiny increase would satisfy this objective, but it is unlikely to satisfy the managers. The objective should be something like, 'increase market share in Europe by 25% by 1990.' Such a statement has a tangible value, which can be compared with other values such as production capacity, market size and number of sales outlets.
3   Is this objective in the interests of the business as a whole? For example, can it be achieved without consuming excessive management time and other resources to the detriment of other parts of the business?
4   Do we have the human resources — if not, can we obtain them? What special skills are needed? Will we need to bring in experts — can they be found?
5   Do we have the financial resources? Will reserves be sufficient for the job or must money be borrowed? Can money be borrowed and at what cost?
6   Have we assessed what the competition will do?
7   Are we satisfied that the information we have is the best we can get? Have we eliminated wishful thinking?

42

8   Have we considered all the alternatives? Would it be better to go for increased sales in South America or the Far East rather than the European areas we have been thinking about?

9   Have we worked out a detailed plan to achieve the objective with built-in contingency action?

A small team of say three or four people, working carefully through this checklist will ensure that the basic thinking behind the venture is sound. Should the answer be 'no' to any question then it is likely that there is a fault in the system. Two or more negative answers indicates a virtual certainty that significant damage will result from continuing with the venture as it stands.

Having worked satisfactorily through the 'clarity checklist' a method will be needed to assess the risk. There are several to choose from.

The Delphi method

This method makes use of the human ability to make judgements but avoids the problem of one powerful personality in a group dominating the thinking of the group. Delphi is particularly helpful when it is recognized that the information available is incomplete or inexact.

Delphi works like this:

1   Select a team of say, six to eight of the most experienced people available (not necessarily the board of directors, many of whom may not have the particular experience required).

2   State the problem clearly to the team, ensuring that everyone has a thorough understanding of the decision to be made.

3   Provide the team with all the relevant facts available and ensure that they understand them. The team should be encouraged to ask questions and to challenge the information. This will assist them to form a view of the value and significance of each item of the data. *N.B.* It

43

must be made clear that no further information can be obtained — either because there is no time to do it or because the information is unobtainable. This prevents the team members from suggesting delaying the decision while more research is done.

4   Allow the team members, say, one hour to consider the problem — *as individuals*. No debate should take place because this may result in opinions being unduly influenced by the more senior or the more dominant people.

5   The team should now be asked to write down on paper (again without reference to each other) their conclusions. For example if three alternative courses of action are being considered they should rank them in order of preference — or reverse order of risk.

6   The 'voting papers' are next collected and the results added up. The result might be:

Action A 4 preferences
Action B 3 preferences
Action C 1 preference

7   The least popular choice, C in the example, is now eliminated and the team is told that it must now choose between A and B. The team should not be told the number of votes for any particular alternative as this may influence their thinking. There are always people who are keen to jump on a bandwagon and this must be avoided.

8   The team is now given say, fifteen minutes individually to reconsider and to vote again.

In most cases a clear majority will emerge for one of the alternatives — if not, an open debate may be necessary, followed by a further secret ballot.

The majority choice should reflect the 'combined wisdom' of the group, only marginally influenced by personal prejudices, and be the lowest risk alternative. If no majority choice emerges, for instance there is an equal preference for each of two alternatives, then it is likely that the risk is closely similar in both cases and the choice must be left to the project leader and his team.

Worst and best — using a spreadsheet

Much time can be wasted in pointless calculation trying to work out a precise value. For example the profit outcome of a venture is a key value which everyone wishes to forecast but it can be a great mistake is to spend time and energy trying to work out the profit figure 'exactly'. Too many senior executives are happy to see a profit forecast of say, £150,250, but are not too happy about a forecast 'within the range £100,000 and £200,000'. Not only is the exact figure likely to be a delusion but it is not necessary to have it! The same decision is likely to be made if the profit forecast is £100,000, £150,000, £200,000 or any figure in between. The risk is not more accurately assessed by insisting on a precise figure.

The practical need is to work out, as well as the information available allows, a feasible range of values for such factors as profit/loss, output, number of customers, supply costs, breakdowns and so on. The problem becomes complex, however, when there are a number of variables each expressed as a range. For example a forecast could include:

Output: within the range 200 — 300 units.
Interest rate: within the range 8% — 11%.
Transport costs: within the range £2 — £3 per ton.

The profit or loss which might arise from the various *combinations* of figures within the ranges may need to be evaluated. For example transport costs of £2.50 per ton combined with an interest rate of 9% may result in a profit. If, however, the interest rate is 9.5% a loss may occur. Alternatively an interest rate of 9.5% may, if combined with a transport cost of £2.1 per ton, result in an attractive profit.

A fairly painless way to deal with this complexity is to use a spreadsheet package on a small computer. Non-computer minded people need not throw up their hands in horror at this suggestion — it really is quite easy. There are a number of spreadsheet packages available which will work on personal computers so no programming or elaborate equipment is required. It is only necessary to have a machine operator who can use the spreadsheet — a typical and versatile one being Lotus 1-2-3 sold by the Lotus Development Corporation.

The data, including all the variables, are written out and the mathematical relationships between them are described. Thus, if there are possible sales volumes of 100, 150 and 200 and possible selling prices of £1, £2 and £3 the sales revenue will be the product of these volumes and prices. This type of information is entered into the computer which can then calculate the various sales revenue figures for a variety of combinations of volume and price. There is nothing complicated about this — indeed, it can be done using pencil and paper. The advantages of using the computer lie in the speed with which the calculations can be done and the arithmetic accuracy which the machine provides.

Using such a system makes it possible to choose a range of least favourable circumstances and work out the result. If the answer is unattractive, *e.g.* the profit result is poor (or even negative) the computer can be asked a series of 'What if' questions. For example, 'What if the sales price is £x?' or 'What if production costs are £n).' Conversely the combination of most optimistic estimates can be fed in and the result worked out. If the profit result (or other objective) does not appear even in the most favourable circumstances then clearly the project is too risky to continue with.

The likelihood is that there is a mix, or a number of mixes, of variables which will suggest a 'go' decision. Judgment can then be exercised in choosing the most feasible or desirable mix. At all events management will know what it must do to succeed in the enterprise and will not be working in the dark. Such calculations have at times demonstrated that a project could *never* succeed whatever was done — thus preventing management from launching into a disaster. They have also sometimes shown that one or two of the variables are much more significant than the others. This enables management to concentrate on these critical aspects and to form a view as to whether they can achieve the values necessary to be successful.

46

Bearing in mind that a 'go' decision should not necessarily depend on a single precise figure but a range, the computer-produced spreadsheet is a convenient way to determine the range or ranges.

Brainstorming

This is another method which makes use of the accumulated wisdom and experience of a group of, say, six to eight people. It differs from the Delphi system in that in brainstorming, the views and ideas of each member of the group are used to stimulate the thinking of the other members.

The brainstorming procedure is as follows:

1   The problem is clearly explained and time taken to ensure that all members of the group have a full and identical understanding of it.
2   The members of the group are asked to call out solutions to the problem as they occur to them. These solutions can be silly or practical, ranging from 'make everyone redundant' to 'try more advertising' — or whatever.

Two things are vitally important: any idea called out must be accepted, and absolutely no comment or criticism from other group members must be allowed. The whole process is designed to create a free flow of ideas and any comment will inhibit this flow. In addition, the 'silly' ideas can (and frequently do) prompt serious and very relevant ideas.

3   The ideas called out are written up on a flip chart paper for all to see. Group members are thus continually reminded of all the ideas already put forward and further thinking is stimulated.
4   When all the ideas have dried up — usually after about twenty minutes, the group, guided by the coordinator, reviews each idea, crossing out all the silly or grossly impractical ones.
5   The remaining list can now be seriously evaluated as a guide to future action.

Brainstorming works well in practice with a high success rate. 'Hopeless' situations have been resolved using it and answers found to 'insoluble' problems. The technique can be used to measure risk by explaining the situation or project to the group and asking them to respond with ideas on one or more questions such as:

•   What can go wrong?
•   How will the market (or competition) react?
•   What will be the reaction of the general public/trade unions/shareholders/employers?

The effect of group thinking in the brainstorming session is to point to risk factors which the originators of the project have overlooked or played down. Used in this way the group is acting as devil's advocate, identifying the risks and their magnitude. Having completed such an exercise the whole thing can be turned on its head and another brainstorming session be used to answer the question, 'How can we reduce or eliminate the risk?' Of course, the project could be so well planned and the risk so low that the group confirms this by not revealing any really significant pitfalls at all.

The criterion comparison method

It is perhaps surprising that businessmen do not often consciously compare a project in a structured way with basic criteria chosen as a matter of policy. Making such a comparison can be an effective form of risk assessment.

The assessment is made by preparing, in advance and in accordance with corporate policy, certain rules which will govern the decisions of the business when any new venture is proposed. These rules, or criteria, must be tailored to the various types of innovation which may be proposed and, for illustration, the following criteria are of the type which might be used when assessing the risk involved in developing and launching a new product:

1   Can the new product provide revenues which reach a

specified level? The level can be expressed as a certain percentage return on capital employed or some other preferred benchmark. One company includes a requirement for the forecast gross profit to be not less than a percentage of the gross profit of the business as a whole. This approach avoids the problem of employing resources on a project which may be profitable but will make no worthwhile difference to the overall fortunes of the business. This is particularly important where a company, over-dependent on one product or market, decides to diversify to obtain greater long-term security. Diversifying into a very limited opportunity, however profitable intrinsically, will do little to solve the long-term problem.

It should be noted that the question is '*Can* the new product reach a specified level', not 'Will . . .'. The problem of deciding whether or not a product *will* reach a certain level of profitability (in a given period of time) is a more complex question. The fundamental acid test is to decide whether or not it is possible at all. A business which neglected to ask this question discovered, too late, that the market available to them was incapable of yielding the expected level of business. Asking the question exposes any risk caused by an absence of adequate research or planning.

2   Will the project absorb more than $x\%$ of the development budget, gross annual earnings, net profit or some other suitable measure? This question is aimed at exposing any risk of a liquidity problem at some stage in the project. A cashflow problem can result in damage to other areas of the business or increased interest charges resulting from the need to borrow more money. The benchmark percentage required is one which has been worked out to ensure that the financial security of the business is not jeopardized by a new venture.

3   Will the project require the use of skilled or specialist manpower to the detriment of other parts of the business? Pulling experienced managers, engineers, salesmen or other key people out of their normal roles

could bring about losses — financial or otherwise — in the mainstream operations of the business.

4 Does the project fit the company image? For example, it is one thing for a building society to diversify into banking operations but quite another to move into estate agency. Surveys have shown that estate agents share bottom place with politicians in the public's esteem. It is strange that building societies should put their public image at risk in this way.

5 How far does the project take the business away from familiar territory and does this meet policy requirements? In other words, will the business find itself in unfamiliar activities where it will be at the mercy of more experienced competitors? Considerable judgement is needed to deal with this problem because the degree of risk will probably be directly related to the degree of unfamiliarity with the new field of activity. Some degree of unfamiliarity may well be acceptable but a carefully considered policy should at least have been made in respect of types of product or service, geographical areas, and type and segment of market.

6 How long will it take to recover the research and development costs? A minimum acceptable period may form part of development policy but this question is also an item for consideration when comparing two alternative proposals.

7 How much time must elapse before growth reaches a pre-determined amount? The project may satisfy profit and percentage of earnings criteria but can the minimum figures be achieved quickly enough? Some criteria for rate of growth may be needed.

8 In the event of failure what will be the additional financial cost of winding up the project? Alongside this question is the important matter of image and reputation. Financial risk may be low but failure may be damaging to the business's reputation.

Examining the experience of others

In the building industry for every 100 bankruptcies another 100 entrepreneurs set up — despite the official bankruptcy statistics which receive ample publicity and should act as a warning. A simple but effective approach for assessing risk is to ask, and answer, the questions (a) has anyone done this or anything closely similar before? and (b) what was the outcome? Examination of other people's previous experience, must, of course, include examination of the way they went about it. Failed ventures not only indicate bad ideas doomed to failure but good ideas which have been mismanaged. Conversely successful ventures may point to the right way to handle a good idea. It can also be helpful to find out the costs incurred by others in carrying out a similar venture — whether or not a successful outcome was achieved.

An interesting example is in the cost of making a takeover bid. There appears to be a relationship between the cost of making the bid and the value of the target business. If a company contemplating making a bid were to research the costs of a few recent examples they would probably find that the *average* cost of a successful bid works out at about 4% of the value. The United Newspapers bid for Fleet for instance cost £15 million against a value of £370 million, *i.e.* 4.05%. Most of the more publicized takeover bids in 1986 cost between 4% and 5% of value. It is also interesting to note that *unsuccessful* bids work out cheaper than successful ones and the average on one small sample taken in 1986 worked out at 1.2% of value. This lower cost is due to lower or nil underwriting costs when the bid fails.

Obtaining the details of previously attempted similar ventures is not as difficult as it may appear at first sight, although some patient research may well be needed. The following potential sources might be tried:

The British Institute of Management survey reports

These reports, which frequently describe the experiences of a sample of British businesses, cover such topics as managing new products and credit management. The BIM also produces occasional papers, books and guides, many of which provide data on management methods used and comment on their merits and demerits.

Financial Times surveys and articles

Reading through a huge pile of back numbers looking for reports and articles on the problem to be solved can be a lengthy and exhausting process. However, it can be well worth the effort.

Trade Association reports

Some trade associations maintain statistical information of interest to their members and publish journals containing articles relevant to the industry concerned. The archives can be helpful and some trade associations will provide help to their members in doing this.

Trying it out

Test marketing is an established method for assessing risk — even if it is not always recognized as such. It makes sense, wherever possible, to proceed with a new product venture in a limited way, such as test marketing to see how the market responds. The result, whether favourable or otherwise, is not however a guarantee of the final outcome if the product is fully launched, because there may be changes in taste or competitor's action in the meantime.

The food industry regularly uses test marketing and often finds that small changes in packaging, appearance or description of their products will greatly increase customer acceptance. Much the same is found in the retail clothing industry where certain branches of a chain store will be used to test customer reaction to a new garment. It should be noted however that both in food and clothing there are marked regional differences in public preferences. Something that sells well in Surrey may not do so in Norfolk or Yorkshire. Test marketing can spot these differences and thus avoid damage.

Not every product or service can be test marketed and not all the risks which businessmen face are matters of product or service. However, if the principle of 'trying it out' is applied in some form or other then the risk element is more easily assessed.

A lesson from the risk assessment experts

There is one industry which is so dependent on its ability to assess risk that selection and use of reliable methods is a fundamental requirement for survival. This industry — insurance — has also had centuries of experience in finding reliable methods. It should be possible for other industries to learn from it.

The popular image of the insurance industry includes the vision of skilled underwriters carefully calculating the levels of premium necessary to yield a profit on insuring everything from bicycles to oil rigs. This image is partly correct. In a few cases such as life and motor insurances a formula approach is used — and the result is frequently wrong. Many insurers in these fields make a loss on their underwriting account and depend upon earnings from investment of premiums to make an overall profit. In reality, over a wide range of situations the underwriter is making an informed guess. An example would be assessing the risk, and calculating the right premium, for towing an oil rig from Korea to the North Sea oil fields. The underwriter will have very little experience to go on since such an event is hardly an everyday occurrence. He will take into account the time of year (is it the hurricane season in the oceans to be crossed?), the value of the rig, the professional reputation of the towing company and other more or less readily accessible information. He will then take a view on how much the customer is likely to be willing to pay and whether or not his competitors (if the broker goes elsewhere) will be keen to take the business. Ultimately he will come up with a figure which includes an allowance for the broker's commission and is to a great extent based on what he thinks he can get away with.

If the oil rig is lost on the voyage he will make a note to double the premium if a similar risk is offered to him again.

One insurer, dealing with regular and repeat business with a claims history to guide premium calculations, uses a form of 'science' and then virtually discards it. The broker first approaches the insurer with the risk, offering his version of what is entailed *i.e.* he will tend to play down any unfavourable aspects. The insurer asks for and records a wide range of facts such as:

- Location of the business
- Value of assets
- Age of the assets
- Age of the business
- Nature of trading done
- Trading area, *i.e.* in which countries
- Claims made during the previous five years

The insurer then records his notion of less tangible attributes such as the quality of the customer's management and his reputation in the industry concerned.

The insurer now makes a lengthy and quite complicated assessment of all the factors he has recorded. For example, if the business is located in a potentially unstable country it will be awarded penalty points. An old established company will be more favourably regarded than a young company and a company trading in say, combustible liquids, will compare unfavourably with one trading in say, steel. All the attributes, including the intangible ones, are given a points rating and these are averaged out. The average, say 1.5 is now applied to a standard premium rate for the type of business concerned which is say, 0.2% of annual turnover.

The premium calculation will then be:

$$1.5 \times 0.2\% \times \textit{annual turnover} = \textit{Premium}$$

This process appears to be, and probably is, a serious attempt to place a mathematical value on the attributes of the customer's business which tend to increase or decrease the

54

risk of a claim. However, the final stage in the process is the one which really counts.

Having worked out the premium the underwriter now takes account of commercial factors. These include:

- The prestige of the customer. Would it be a feather in the insurer's cap to have this company on their books? If so, the premium could be reduced.
- Whether or not the premium, as calculated, is likely to be attractive to the customer. If it is feared that he might find cheaper insurance elsewhere, possibly overseas, the premium will be reduced accordingly.
- Whether or not the customer is a company which is part of a group of companies and there is a chance that the rest of the group can be won over. Again, if this is the case the premium may be reduced.
- Whether or not the customer is likely to have difficulties in obtaining suitable insurance elsewhere — he may for instance be a company resident in an underdeveloped country with limited or unsophisticated domestic insurance facilities. If so, the premium may be increased.

The underwriting process is therefore an assessment of risk which starts with as much factual and opinion-based information as possible, continues with a mathematical treatment of the facts and ends with a commercial judgement. If the mathematical treatment was absolutely dependable then there could be only one premium figure which is acceptable. In reality there is a range of premium levels which will satisfy the underwriter whose final decisions are dominated by judgement. The lesson is obvious.

Summary

1   While it makes sense to collect and analyse as much information as possible relating to the proposed change or venture it is not realistic to base decisions on purely mathematical methods.

2   More reliable methods of risk assessment involve the use of judgment and the combined wisdom of experienced people — taking full account of all the information available.

3   The problem to be solved must be clearly stated and understood before any sensible decision can be made using judgment-based techniques.

4   Pseudo-accuracy should be avoided: it wastes time and gives a false sense of certainty.

5   The industry which is most concerned with risk assessment — insurance — depends on the judgment-based techniques.

Part III

Making the Decision

Chapter 5

Weighing the pros and cons

Whatever methods are used to assess the risk, scientific, hunch or a sensible mixture, a point is reached where a decision must be taken whether to go or not to go. The decision will involve careful consideration of the results of the assessment methods used and will also involve reducing to a minimum any irrational emotional influences. The latter aspect is dealt with in Chapter 6. In this chapter we will look at some of the ways to come to a final decision, starting with the question of *who* should be given the job of making this decision. This may appear to be scarcely worthy of discussion but in far too many cases the wrong decision is taken simply because the wrong people take it. Although it can be argued that in important cases the board of directors should examine the facts and reach a conclusion, it can also be the case that boards of directors talk too much about matters in which they have no first-hand or recent experience. A good chairman can ensure that the board sticks to the point and does not become bogged down in irrelevant matters but even then there is a chance of wasting time (at best) and making the wrong decision (at worst).

Another problem with using the board is that often the key people are excluded. In one such case a middle management executive had studied a problem, worked out a solution and prepared a report. The solution involved taking a particular course of action which the board debated and rejected. The executive was not invited to be present at the board meeting and the decision was taken solely on the basis of the report. At least one director had not read the report prior to the meeting on the grounds that since he knew the proposed action to be wrong he did not need to waste time on the details! The content of the report received little attention from the directors who, concentrating on the action proposed and not the reasons for it, were putting themselves in a poor position to reach a sensible conclusion. Had the executive been given the opportunity to present his evidence and draw the board's attention to the significance of certain facts the outcome might have been very different. In this case the company concerned missed a golden opportunity which was profitably exploited by a foreign competitor some time later.

The referral of important matters to a high level can therefore transfer the decision-making process away from the people who are sufficiently close to the problem truly to understand it. However, the board of directors cannot abdicate its responsibility for the good management of the business and practical methods must be found to maintain proper control, while avoiding bad decisions based on remoteness or lack of day-to-day experience.

One method used very successfully by an international business involves delegation within pre-determined limits. The business concerned is frequently faced with risk problems of a financial nature — some requiring very rapid action. Difficulties were encountered in earlier years in obtaining decisions from a board which could not meet frequently enough to deal with the flow of decisions required. The board had operated a system where the managers requiring the decision attended the meeting and presented the facts, but this in turn created delay and extra work. To make a proper presentation required the preparation of visual aids, executive summaries and the like, and the meetings — which tended to be lengthy — consumed the time not only of the directors but also of the managers.

Realizing that this method of dealing with the work was inefficient, the board decided to delegate all decisions of a routine nature. The company's definition of routine was any transaction less than £50,000 in value. The maintenance of control was achieved by delegating such transactions to the managers handling the business *plus* either the chairman or his deputy. In practice the managers involve the chairman or deputy at a relatively early stage by memorandum or discussion which not only informs them of developments but also gives them the opportunity to feed in their own ideas and advice. When the time comes to make the decision these board representatives are already familiar with many of the pros and cons and have already satisfied themselves that policy considerations have been given proper attention. The final decisions, which are made quickly and with demonstrably greater success, are recorded over the weeks and reported to the full board at the next regular meeting thus keeping all the directors informed of the way things are going. Board members have found this cumulative reporting a better way to assess what is going on than the earlier method where individual problems were dealt with in isolation. The broader picture presented provides a more accurate and indicative guide as to how the business is going.

The major risks, where more than £50,000 is involved, are still presented to the board as a whole so that more control is applied where the risk is greater. Time and effort have been saved and the success rate is higher following the introduction of this approach. Pareto's Principle (10% of the transactions cause 90% of the work) applied in this case as the great bulk of the decisions related to the lower value risks.

The principle of delegation is an important one if paralysis is to be avoided. Delegation can also assist in placing the decision-taking role with the people who have the knowledge required to come to the right conclusion. Not least in value is the motivating effect of delegation, there being nothing more demoralizing to creative people in a business than to have their ideas sat on, watered down or unduly delayed by a body which is actually or believed to be remote from the scene of action.

Alternative ways to delegate are:

- To the company development team (if there is one, see Chapter 8).
- To heads of divisions or departments.
- To a team of two or three senior people — one of whom is a director.
- Some permutation or variation of the above.

The guiding principle should be to encourage decision and risk taking at a level as close to the action as possible. The right level and the right type of people will vary from business to business but the principle must be adhered to. There never has been, or ever will be, a managing director or other chief executive with a monopoly of genius.

There are, in addition, a number of delegation traps to watch out for. Decision takers should not, except in the most critical circumstances, do any of the following:-

1   Hand the whole thing over to a firm of outside consult-ants. It is *most* unlikely that an outside consultancy will know your business better than you do although they may have previous experience of a problem which you are facing for the first time. There is merit in asking a consultant to give you his opinion and advice on special-ized subjects by joining the debate for a few hours or a day. If the whole problem is given to consultants, you will face delay and a sizeable bill.

2   Form a special committee to study the problem. Time will be lost while they arrange their first meeting, agree their terms of reference, organize more fact finding and generally create work all round. If the problem had been clearly identified and described in the first place a decision should have been made and appointing a committee is merely a convenient way to duck responsibility.

3   Defer the decision until everyone is less busy — that day will never come.

The worst that can happen

A useful benchmark in weighing the pros and cons is the estimate of the worst scenario (see Chapter 4). If the worst that can reasonably be expected to happen in terms of profit (or loss), public reaction or company reputation is acceptable, then there is no problem in deciding whether or not to go ahead. In other words the damage done by a total failure may be so little that there is, in terms of the definition in Chapter 1, no risk at all. It is important however, in such a case, to be sure that all the worst factors which have been included in the calculation have been realistically stated. The figures for the lowest level of sales, highest price for raw materials and so on which were included in the spreadsheet should be reconsidered and, if necessary, the analysis re-run. This is not an exhortation to keep going over the figures endlessly — a process which leads nowhere — but a reminder that when the range of possible results is favourable even at the worst extreme, care must be taken to ensure that undue optimism has not crept in somewhere.

It is also possible that the most *favourable* scenario produces an unacceptable result and once again a decision should not be difficult although, again, a quick once-over of the figures may be worthwhile.

What is an acceptable loss?

Referring again to the definition in Chapter 1, the objective should be to avoid significant damage. What is significant to one person or business is not necessarily significant to another. How can the acceptability or otherwise of a possible level of damage be determined? Once again the insurance industry offers a guide in the form of the deductible or excess used in insurance contracts. The deductible is that part of each loss which is borne by the insured company not by the insuring company. Suppose for example a manufacturing company insures itself, among other things, for product liability and theft. The company may consider that its products are well designed, carefully inspected and have a long history

63

of satisfactory and safe performance. This being the case the company may feel that there is only a very slight chance of claims being made on them for product liability but, if they occur they are likely to be large. The company would not expect a continuous flow of small liability claims to be made on them as a result say, of product defect.

In this case the company would argue that since premium costs are reduced for the larger deductible they should opt for as high a figure as possible. The problem is knowing how high to go. This question is most readily answered by posing another question: 'What is the maximum loss that we could suffer without damaging the business beyond repair?' If the answer is £10,000, then taking a safety margin of 100%, the company might opt for a deductible of £5,000. It will of course also have in hand, as a contribution to any losses, the money saved as a result of reducing the premium to be paid.

The theft risk is an entirely different one where the acceptable deductible is likely to be much lower. The chance of theft is much higher than the chance of a product liability claim, but the size of each loss will probably be much lower. The decision on deductible levels in the case of theft is therefore primarily one of considering the cumulative effect of a number of small losses. A much lower deductible will probably be chosen, say £100, on the basis that the company can absorb a number of losses up to this level but needs protection against say, five or six losses of £1,000 each. In addition the company must consider a high limit of cover if, for instance, they deal in small size valuables such as radios, whisky or leather goods. These are items which, being easily sold, are attractive to thieves who may steal a whole lorry or container load. Such a loss could be catastrophic to a small company.

A question to be asked in determining acceptability will therefore be, 'What will be the financial effect on the business?' Acceptability does not depend solely on financial considerations, however, and it may be necessary to consider other types of loss, such as damage to the company reputation, which can result in a fall in share price or a less favourable credit rating.

Looking at the worst that can happen is a benchmark

method for deciding whether to go ahead or not — combined with agreement on the maximum acceptable loss.

What happens if we do nothing?

There are some cases where it is safer to do nothing, but normally only when the chance of successful action is very slim. The fact that a change is proposed at all normally means that either an opportunity has presented itself or a problem has appeared. New ideas are usually stimulated by some form of pressure. Walking away from the decision may be the easiest thing to do but it is likely that by doing so the original opportunity or problem will still be there — and may be potentially dangerous if ignored.

A neglected opportunity may be exploited by a competitor and a problem may get worse if nothing is done about it. Any serious proposal to do nothing should therefore be very carefully weighed up and the following questions asked and answered:

1   Will our competitors have a chance to gain an advantage?
2   Will there be any long-term damage to the company instead of, or additional to, any short-term effects?
3   Will the problem get worse?
4   Will we be faced with the same decision later — with less time to act?
5   Has our decision to do nothing resulted from poor work resulting in an inadequate plan of action? Can a better plan be worked out which *is* acceptable?

Failure to act is too frequently based on complacency, lack of courage or an inadequate appreciation of the situation. Conversely, if the position is so uncertain that a decision to go ahead amounts to a sheer gamble then there would be no merit in it, unless to keep things as they are is certain disaster.

A junior executive, knowing that the status quo was damaging, but not being able to decide which course of action to take, did nothing. His boss, more than a little annoyed at this inaction said to him, 'No action meant certain trouble so even if you did not know which choice to make you should have acted.'

The compromise solution

A company can find itself in a position where the very life of the business is threatened. This can result from new technology exploited by competitors plus perhaps an ageing product line which can no longer hold its own in the market. In such cases, and those where too many suppliers are chasing too little business, a decision must be taken whether or not to:

- Soldier on and hope for the best.
- Update the product line.
- Invest in new technology to reduce costs.
- Diversify.
- Close down and cut the losses.

The first of these alternatives is too much like wishful thinking to be regarded, by professional businessmen, as a serious contender. The last alternative is a despairing though sometimes realistic course of action. In most cases the decision to be made will involve the other alternatives, all of which are likely to be expensive and full of risk.

Updating the product line will require market research, design work, retooling and retraining, advertising and so on. All of these are costly and there is always the chance that having spent the money the result will be a flop. Investing in new technology can mean substantial capital expenditure, and diversification takes research time and financial commitment which might include the possibility of buying another business to obtain the product, market and know-how.

These options then, are expensive and managements might prefer to look for cheaper, compromise solutions. Such solutions may be available, but care must be taken to avoid opting for one which does not deal adequately with the risk but merely puts off the crisis for another year or two. For example, short-term survival may be achieved by one or more measures such as:

1 Reducing the work force to save money and so cut unit production costs. This, unless very substantial in scope, is unlikely to be of any great or lasting value. Cutting a little wages cost here and there must not be confused with wholesale elimination of uneconomic activities.

2 Abandoning the less profitable markets, making such overhead savings as are possible and concentrating resources on the remaining markets. This option must be carefully examined to ensure that overhead costs can be cut sufficiently to make a real difference. It is normally the case that real savings in manpower, plant, buildings and other costs only arise if the pull-out from a market represents a large fall in production and a large fall in the number of transactions handled. It is far more likely that the same buildings must be retained but with less use made of them and that production facilities will still be required but at lower capacity.

   Savings can of course be made in sales, advertising, insurance and perhaps stockholding, but unless there are resources wholly dedicated to the market to be abandoned the total is not likely in most cases to be significant.

   Another way of looking at this option is to consider the contribution to fixed costs that a non-profitable market may provide. Unless, as already indicated, those fixed costs can be reduced or eliminated it may be better to keep things as they are. Only if the revenue from the market concerned is less than the marginal cost of the business done is there a clear case for pulling out. Even then it must be remembered that abandoning a market will not be forgotten by customers, agents and others. If ever there is a wish to return to that market it will be difficult.

3 Abandoning the less profitable products. Much the same considerations apply as in the case of abandoning a market and it is necessary to ensure that real savings

67

will result and that these savings will have a significant effect.

Notwithstanding the warnings given above, such action may be valuable in providing a breathing space, and may create funds for innovation. Even if profits, or extra profits, are guaranteed for only a short time, enough liquidity may be built up to finance expansion in more promising directions. Even a carefully considered cut-back which is not followed by a subsequent expansion, however, could be the death of the business.

What is done and the way it is done is a reflection of the attitude of the decision takers to risk. The experience and attitude of Lansing, the largest UK forklift truck makers, gives food for thought.

Lansing, the sixth largest producer of lift trucks in the western world, were faced in 1986 with severe pressures. Markets had been depressed for some time and cheap competition from abroad had made itself felt. Lansing could have decided on a cut-back in the face of these problems but instead decided on a £14 million investment programme. The purpose was to improve production efficiency and as a result cut product costs by 15%. A new production system was designed to reduce production time by two thirds and to improve quality. The thinking behind this move is exemplified by the words of a company spokesman reported in the press at the time. 'This is not a survival plan — it is a plan for prosperity.' The lesson for those weighing up the pros and cons is to be courageous — attack is often the best form of defence.

Leader or follower

From time to time managements weighing up the pros and cons are dealing with a proposal involving a product, a service or perhaps a particular way to do business which is entirely new. Research may have resulted in a new material, a new technology or an entirely new product for which there is no previous experience. There is, for many people, a particular attraction in being first in the field with something new. The unique product may sweep the board and establish a permanent and substantial lead over any competitive effort. What, in reality, does it mean to be a leader? Is it a pro or con?

Forty years ago there was the first ball point pen, the Biro. This innovation was marketed at first as a high-tech product and was retailed at a high price to the upper segment of the market. It was not long before the same technology was copied by competitors and marketed in a cheaper form. In due course the market was taken over by the cheaper product which eventually included the mass production throwaway model. No doubt Biro invested money in research and product development and took the additional risk of introducing a new idea to a market dominated by the long established and familiar nib pen. In this case the pioneer made a fortune from his innovation, but it is clear that the followers have also done well.

There is a more recent example which demonstrates that a leader can do well but a follower, in some respects at least, can do even better. This example is found in the world of the small computer where Amstrad, a company which began by selling car aerials in 1968, reported sales of £300 million (and profits of £75 million) in 1986 — from the sale of small computers. In about two years Amstrad went from nil sales to the supplier selling more small computers in Britain than anyone else. All this was done as a follower.

Amstrad examined the small computer market and spotted a demand for a machine within the price range attractive to the small business, the sole trader and the private individual. A leading existing product was carefully analysed and an equally effective substitute produced at a lower price. The price reduction was achieved by finding ways and means to reduce production costs.

Amstrad did not make any brilliant inventions but did look closely at the needs of the customers and used the pioneering work of others to establish themselves in a growing market.

A leader who got it wrong was RCA, one of the great trail blazers in the USA. Backed up by a successful history of development in mass radio and black and white television, RCA put twenty years of research into the videodisc. This pioneering effort was a disastrous failure which contributed significantly to the decline of the business which was ultimately taken over by General Electric.

There are a number of varying opinions as to why the videodisc failed while its rival the video recorder was a worldwide success. Some experts point to the videodisc's inability to record television programmes, others say it entered the market too late (the VCR was an already established rival). Price was, on the face of it, an advantage to RCA which produced a machine retailing at about $500, as opposed to the VCRs which were on the market at more than double this amount. However, with the wisdom and benefit of hindsight it has been pointed out that the dealers were not enthusiastic about pushing the low priced product since they earned more money from the high priced alternative. In due course VCRs came down in price which, whatever the attitude of the dealers, reduced or removed RCA's price advantage.

It is ironic that RCA carried out plenty of market research and with strong support from some parts of the company went so far as to develop its own VCR. It seems that this idea was shot down in an internal battle over what was the best thing to do. The technical research people, who supported the videodisc, gained supremacy over those in the company who were more clearly aware of the market and its preferences and needs. The technical research side of RCA was much favoured by the chief executive and it seems that his patronage resulted in technological investment gaining ascendancy over common sense and good marketing. Being a leader in the field is therefore by no means a guarantee of a great and profitable future.

The lessons to be learned from these examples are:

1   Whether a leader or a follower, paying attention to the market and its needs is of paramount importance.
2   A follower can successfully exploit a gap in the market without putting any technological development costs at risk.
3   Management must ensure that particular disciplines

within the company do not dominate the conduct of new projects. A balanced view must be taken.

Once again it is necessary to consider the definition of risk and to concentrate on the 'significant damage' point. If, in order to be a leader, a great deal of research and development cost is anticipated then, regardless of any other factor, the effect of this cost on the business as a whole must be taken into account. Spending proportionately large sums to the detriment of the rest of the business is dangerous. This is gambling and not the business of the serious entrepreneur with any sense of responsibility. The fact that the proposal may be fiercely promoted by the company's technical whizz kids is not necessarily sufficient reason to go ahead. Decision takers must ensure that market evidence also supports the scheme.

A problem or an opportunity

There seems to be a natural tendency among businessmen to spend a disproportionate amount of their time on problems, rather than on opportunities. As a result, decision taking on a new course of action is not infrequently a matter of consideration of a way to resolve a problem.

The first question to ask is, 'Are we right in concentrating on this problem. Is there no opportunity that should be exploited using the same resources?'

One manufacturer of plastics repeatedly spent large sums to improve the efficiency of production of a loss-making product. Various schemes were tried out and new machinery installed. Service to customers was stressed on the marketing side, but this led to acceptance of absurdly small orders which added further to the production costs. The facts were that:

1   The market was oversupplied.
2   Competitors had entered the market with more efficient manufacturing methods and on a larger scale.
3   The major competitors could use any surplus manufacturing capacity for the production of other products.

71

4   At least one major competitor also produced the raw
     materials and enjoyed the benefit of vertical integration.

   Each time a new scheme came up for approval the
expense was examined solely within the parochial limits of
the factory concerned. Money and effort was repeatedly
poured into the problem when it would have been better to
recognise defeat and concentrate on developing an alternative
product. The plant was eventually closed with no alternative
product developed.

Summary

1   It is important to ensure that decisions in a risk situ-
     ation are taken by the right people — that is, those in
     the best position to make informed judgements. It is not
     necessarily right for decision taking to be a monopoly of
     the board of directors.
2   There are ways to delegate decision taking without loss
     of control by the board or the involvement of directors.
     A number of alternatives are given. However, there are
     forms of pseudo-delegation which must be avoided.
3   A useful benchmark test is to work out the worst and
     best results of the project.
4   Acceptable loss can be assessed as the damage to the
     business which can be absorbed.
5   Doing nothing is rarely the best alternative and is
     frequently dangerous.
6   In some cases a compromise solution may be found —
     at least to achieve short-term survival in a critical situ-
     ation. There are difficulties and dangers in this
     approach but with careful control and the right attitude
     a compromise can provide a way out of trouble.
7   Being a leader — that is, to be first in the field with a
     new product — is attractive to many and can be a
     winning situation. The follower can be equally or more
     successful, but in both cases close attention to the
     market is a must!
8   Too much management effort and money is expended

on problems while opportunities are neglected. Exploiting the opportunity is a better bet.

Chapter 6

The human factor

So far we have considered the various forms of risk, and ways and means to combine calculated hunch with the scientific approach. Reference was made in Chapter 1 to the human factor which, regardless of how much research is done, is probably the single most important element in risk taking. These human factors, normally exemplified in sincerely held and honestly expressed beliefs, require close attention both by individuals and by management teams since they can cause irrational action. Individuals must try to recognize limitations created by their own background, training or personality. Management as a whole must equally be aware of group or individual attitudes. It is therefore necessary to take account of the influences affecting the potential members when forming the decision-taking team. There will be a variety of motivating influences, including almost all of the seven deadly sins! However let us start by examining the influence of two particular professions where the nature of the training given to practitioners influences their willingness to take risks.

The accountant's approach

The standard methods used by accountants to evaluate revolutionary changes in manufacturing systems are based on thinking developed before the first world war. At that time machinery, materials and the arithmetic of labour costs were very different from those of the 1980s. These out-of-date accounting methods ignore the financial effect of reducing inventories and take no account of modern management considerations such as customer service, quality standards and employee welfare. The old notion of pay-back time is also being seriously questioned as a result of Japanese experience. In a paper entitled *Accounting Lag: The Obsolescence of Cost Accounting Systems*, Robert Kaplan has challenged the traditional cost accounting approach. Professor Kaplan maintains that the accountants' methods do not provide useful indicators for managing production systems and the obsolescence of the procedures is an obstacle to proper decision making.

These are manufacturing-orientated complaints, but they have their counterparts in other areas. Accountants use 'book values' to decide the market value of an item to be sold. The accountant who insists that the book value must at least be equalled by the selling price is ignoring two facts:

1   The selling price is determined by what buyers are willing and able to pay — not the book value.
2   It is better to enjoy the proceeds of having the cash than it is to hang on to an item yielding nothing until the accountant has written it down to the price that can be obtained.

This out of date thinking exemplifies the possible approach that an accountant may take to risk situations. He may be more anxious than most businessmen to avoid risk. The accountant, by virtue of his professional status, can influence decision-taking teams away from an opportunity.

Accountants are as much concerned with costs as they are with profits. The greater the costs associated with a project and hence the greater the damage resulting from failure, the greater will be the accountant's concern. He therefore seeks the alternative which minimizes the potential loss and this is rarely the alternative which offers a high return. The ability to handle risk is a managerial skill far removed from the security-seeking world of the accountant whose whole training is geared to certainty. Accountants are sometimes heard to complain of the rashness and carelessness of non-accounting colleagues and there is often justification for these complaints, but the cautious attitude of the accountant should not be allowed to dominate decision taking.

Risk taking is unavoidable if progress is be made. Everyone concerned with it should be able and willing to overcome any unjustified conservative bias. In *The Risk Takers* Richard Branson is reported as saying, 'If you sit down with accountants and look at profit and loss projections, they'll manage to come up with all sorts of reasons why something won't work. Well, I think if you've got a gut feeling about something the trial and error can produce the best results.'

The lawyer's approach

Lawyers tend, like accountants, to seek the known position. They are trained to do so, and trained to give advice which takes account of even the remotest possibility of something going wrong.

In almost every business activity there is a potential legal risk. Product liability, third party liability and the dangers of infringing various Acts are always present. A lawyer's warnings about the Consumer Safety Act, the Trades Description Act, the Sale of Goods Act and the like can be frightening if not seen in perspective. There is always a chance of infringement of an Act or of breaching a contract due to ignorance, error or neglect, but these are reasons for taking due care but not for abandoning the project.

The influences of these two professions both encourage an over-cautious approach. There are, conversely, other roles which tend to encourage impetuous attitudes, especially, for example, salesmen. A study carried out in the USA and reported in *Taking Risks* by MacCrimmon & Wehrung came to the not very surprising conclusion that older managers are more cautious than younger ones. However, MacCrimmon & Wehrung also concluded that junior managers were more cautious than senior managers, which suggests that acquiring seniority balances the impetuousness of youth and hence job security may be a factor to consider. The more senior manager, although probably older, is less likely to be fired for a mistake than his junior colleagues and may therefore take a more confident view.

These reactions to risk are of course also prompted by more basic human instincts of which decision takers should be aware both in themselves and in others.

Instincts and attitudes

Complacency

No company however successful can afford to adopt a complacent attitude, but it tends to develop in companies, and individuals, with a track record of success. This leads in turn, to a tendency to brush aside any threats to the business. One such case became apparent in 1984 when a company, long established and the leader in its field, became aware of a newly formed competitor. The newcomer was strongly backed, being an off-shoot of another very successful business. The press reported the arrival of the newcomer with enthusiasm as they sensed a fierce battle which would provide ample exciting copy for articles on the subject. For some months little was heard from the threatened company whose chief executive dismissed the newcomer as of no consequence. No action was taken to fend off the threat and the valuable few months between press announcements and the actual launch of the newcomer were wasted. The new company, which had very carefully prepared its attack on the market, made an immediate impact and, too late, its competitors recognized the dangers. Important customers switched loyalties in the first few months, other announced their intention of doing so when existing contracts had expired and long-neglected markets were successfully penetrated by the newcomer.

The first reaction of the now seriously worried company was to publicly denigrate the newcomer and a campaign of 'dirty tricks' was started. This campaign was so transparent that it proved counter-productive — more customers changed sides. Eventually the threatened company began to improve its product and service, which had been long neglected over the years when a virtual monopoly had been enjoyed. This action was too late and also counter-productive. Disgruntled customers now became even more aware of the former inadequacies of the company.

Within a year the newcomer had captured the best customers and the older company started a cost-cutting campaign to counteract falling revenues. Spacious offices were closed down and the staff rehoused in cramped and dreary premises. This, and the fact that the staff could readily see the direction in which things were going, brought about a sharp drop in morale and the departure of some key people. This downward spiral effect went on until the business was sold off. The whole process, from becoming aware of the threat to selling the business, took only two years, demonstrating how dangerous complacency can be.

The action necessary to counteract complacency which the above mentioned company should have adopted includes:

1   Refusal to believe that even when dominant in the market no improvements to product or service can be made or are necessary. Developments must be constantly sought and pursued — always from the viewpoint of the customers and their needs.
2   Treating all actual or potential threats very seriously and regularly assessing the quality and activities of the opposition.
3   Being prepared to react promptly, positively and imaginatively to any change in circumstances representing either a problem or an opportunity.
4   Regarding any complacent feelings as the symptoms of a fatal disease. The 'It can't happen to me' syndrome is an ideal way for soldiers to keep their sanity in battle but does not remove the risk of a bullet in the brain.

Ambition

Ambition can be a powerful driving force which, when properly channelled and controlled, can result in creative and beneficial progress both for the individual and the company. It can also run out of control and blind people to the realities of life.

Strong ambition tends to overcome the sensible level of caution required in all business decisions and can encourage impetuous activity. Balance is required to mix the motivating effect of individual and corporate ambition with a methodical and, as far as possible, fact-based approach.

Ambition can overcome good judgment when a poor idea is strongly promoted by an ambitious individual who sees it as an opportunity for personal advancement. The formation of a new subsidiary business was fought for by an executive who hoped and expected that he would be appointed chief executive to run it. All the evidence showed that the idea was a bad one and fortunately for the company and the individual the plan was turned down. The executive himself realized some months later that he had been wrong, recognized that his ambitions had dulled his critical sense and acknowledged that had the scheme gone ahead with himself in charge he would have suffered most as a result.

Expanding a business with disproportionate increases in fixed costs is another trap for the ambitious. A sole proprietor furniture business was progressing steadily and making good profits. The owner worked in the business himself with four employees and operated from modest premises in an unfashionable area. He was eager to expand and took new and more expensive premises with a view to expanding the staff and entering the mass-produced furniture market. His enthusiasm for growth clouded his judgment and prevented him from realizing what he was heading for.

His existing business was founded on high quality products made to order. In this field he was successful despite a limited market. He was right in his belief that to expand he had to move into the mass-produced market which offered many more customers, but he overlooked the competition he would face.

The fixed cost of the rent for the new premises could not adequately be met with revenue from the existing business and he was unable to develop the new business in time before his financial reserves ran out. His ambition had prevented him from calculating his chances of breaking into a new market already served by a number of much larger and well established suppliers.

If he had been less ambitious, this entrepreneur might have begun developing his new products in existing premises and built up a customer base slowly. Winning a small contract or two in the mass market could have given him the funds to take on the larger fixed costs. Alternatively he might have expanded by diversification into something outside the furniture industry.

This mistake of taking on disproportionate fixed costs is by no means limited to sole proprietors or other small businesses. Large offices and factories have been taken on by companies with ambitions which exceed their resources, revenues and common sense.

Sloth

Sometimes disguised as the prudent exercise of caution, sloth can be a killer. There are always reasons to be found for inactivity and quite a few business executives are experts at finding them. The owner of a printing business was a master of this form of disguise and rather than investigate more modern machinery or seek new business he was content to allow himself to be put out of business by more up-to-date and vigorous competitors. He actually ended up working as a machine operator for one of his competitors!

Sloth is a vice to which no one will admit but there are clues to its existence. The symptoms include:

1   Short working hours on the part of senior executives.
2   Long, unproductive boardroom lunches.
3   Delaying tactics in dealing with ideas from younger executives.
4   The formation of committees and sub-committees to talk endlessly about ideas. With sufficient committees the slothful boss can get rid of virtually any matter indefinitely.
5   The absence of any form of long-term strategy or objectives.

6   Close and continuous attention to trivia.
7   An obsession with status symbols including under-employed secretaries.
8   High turnover rates among the more able and ambitious staff.

Naturally any one of these symptoms can be caused by something other than sloth but a combination of two or three is a warning.

Sloth is caused by lack of motivation for which there can be a variety of causes, including complacency at senior levels of management and lack of ambition. This indicates how closely linked are the various attitudes of those who must face risks and make decisions.

Greed

Greed is a powerful motivator which is perhaps the most likely to dull the senses. In the heyday of Investors Overseas Services (once one of the world's biggest financial empires) the charismatic founder Bernie Cornfeld motivated his salesmen by stimulating their greed.

'Do you sincerely want to be rich?' was his battle-cry to rooms crammed with excited young sales associates. 'Yes!' was the answer roared back by the audience who then went out into the streets to sell yet more financial plans and earn yet more commission.

The same technique was used to sell shares in IOS Ltd to the company employees in the UK when IOS went public in 1969. At a meeting of enthusiastic employees in a hall in Wembley, the greed of some was sufficient to lead them to buy many more shares than they could afford — including a young couple who put all their savings into the offer. When the company failed, the shares became worthless. They lost almost all they had, including a hard-earned deposit for their first home.

The more prudent employees sold their shares immediately and made a good profit. The greedier ones held on hoping for an even higher price and lost the lot.

81

Greed then, can tempt the individual and the group into a high-risk situation. As everyone in business knows, promises of high rewards should be examined very closely, but human nature is such that this caution is frequently set aside. When considering the risk in a proposal it is important to remember that the higher the potential reward the greater the risk is likely to be, and not allow greed to take over.

Fear

The accountant, as well as being influenced towards caution by his training is also subject to fear. He shares this fear with any specialist in a team of decision takers because the specialist is the most vulnerable person if things go wrong. 'You are the expert', says the chairman with the willing agreement of his generalist colleagues. 'You should have spotted this weakness. That is what we pay you for.'

The fact that at the time of the decision the entire team agreed with the specialist will be forgotten. In this way decision taking may be influenced not by the inherent risk in the proposal but by the risk to the individuals. MacCrimmon & Wehrung have concluded that managers are more cautious when considering a proposition which affects their personal finances.

Blame or financial loss are not the only causes of fear.

Status loss

Switching investment from one product division to another will be vigorously opposed by the director who will be in charge of a shrinking empire.

Job loss

If the new project fails the people handling it may not be taken back into the company. They may disappear along with the scheme.

Reputation loss

This is often founded on the 'not invented here' attitude which discourages support for someone else's idea. The fear is that the originator of the idea will, if the scheme succeeds, grow in reputation. The opponent fears that his own reputation will be lowered by comparison.

Fear is thus not limited to fears about the proposal but includes the purely personal aspects relating to the individuals involved.

Pride

This emotion comes in two forms — the acceptable form of pride such as in a job well done or in the good reputation of one's company, and the other form which corrupts. This latter form, seen in the haughty, pompous executive, can be extremely damaging to the progress of a business.

Apart from offending other people a proud attitude can rob the business of some very good ideas. The problem is most marked in companies with a very formal organizational structure and a very hierarchal environment. What is most often lost is the good idea put forward by a junior employee.

The junior employee who has spotted what he thinks is a good idea will try to promote it. The proud executive will kill it by one or more ways. The first way is to prevent the idea going beyond the proud executive's desk, either by rejecting it out of hand or by sending it back for further thought. The emotion behind this move is that of not believing that someone else, particularly a junior, could actually have a good idea. This opinion is often sincerely held and not only is it a gross form of self-delusion but it can also be costly to the business.

One expert at this form of idea-blocking would always insist on a written proposal. This gave him the opportunity to face the proposer with the document held delicately by one corner, between finger and thumb. He would suspend the document with arm outstretched about twelve inches above his desk whilst he remained seated. With an expression which clearly suggested that the document was contaminated with a smelly and grossly unpleasant substance he would say, 'I don't think this sort of thing is really for us, do you?' Thus without any assessment of the risk in the new idea, the proposal was killed off at birth. The proposer of the scheme would retire defeated and hurt, vowing never to use his brains for the company again.

Should an idea from a junior actually escape the proud executive's first line of defence and reach a group of people for consideration the proud executive will continue the battle. He will not deal with the idea on its merits but will use any means, however unreasonable, to destroy it. The methods include discrediting the originator of the idea.

All this may sound exaggerated but it really does happen. The proud executive is usually clever enough not to allow his motives to show and he will produce plausible, if invalid, objections. On one occasion a proud executive killed an idea by stating that it involved doing business with people whose honesty and integrity were doubtful and the scheme thereby very risky. In reality the unacceptable people were in no way involved or likely to be but the other decision takers did not find that out until too late.

One company which positively encourages ideas from within is 3M, which was described by Peters & Waterman in their book *In Search of Excellence* as 'marked by barely organized chaos surrounding its product champions.' 3M promotes entrepreneurial activity in which someone with an idea is encouraged to develop it (albeit with careful monitoring). The result: some significant successes including the simple, low-risk and very successful Post-It self-stick notes. We all survived for years without them but now every office has them.

Since these are all human reactions and feelings they can never be totally eliminated, and purely objective behaviour will never be achieved. However, awareness of the instincts and attitudes which may lie behind the expressed views of decision takers goes some way to encouraging objectivity. Self-examination is a course open to all even if the motives of colleagues cannot be accurately analyzed, allowed for or countered.

Ignorance

A great weakness in dealing with risk is ignorance of any important aspect of the scheme or the influences on it. Mention has already been made (and will be made again) of the need to collect the relevant information, but the story does not stop there. The information collected is not always easy to interpret. If the decision-making team lack specialist advice on a particular subject they should obtain it.

A classic failure to interpret the facts occurred some years ago and still has an effect on the actions of certain businesses. This failure, in which greed was linked with ignorance, concerned the computer leasing and insurance industries.

Computers, in a world where technical advance is rapid, are prone to rapid obsolescence. Lessors of computers were finding that lessees wanted to cancel contracts for particular models of machines in order to replace them with the latest versions. The lessors, recognizing a problem, approached the insurance market and asked them for insurance against financial loss arising from a lessee wishing to change machines before the leasing contract expired. The insurers were only too pleased to take on this business which was part of a major growth area. The result was a disaster for the insurers because their ignorance of the nature of computers was such that they did not realize that obsolescence was almost inevitable and the very existence of the insurance cover was an invitation for lessor and lessee to change machines. Losses were substantial — as any junior programmer or trainee systems analyst could have foreseen. This painful experience still has its effects in that years later certain underwriters are still frightened of anything to do with computers, even when, in insurance terms, the risk is a good one. Sadly, the ignorance is still there.

The 'well-known fact' syndrome

All well-known facts should be treated with the greatest suspicion since they are trotted out by the person with no real evidence to support his views. Well-known facts often represent wishful thinking or prejudice and have no place in the assessment of risk or the decision-making process.

For many centuries it was a well-known fact that the world was flat and that the sun revolved round the earth. Intelligent men risked their lives by challenging the second of these beliefs, which was fundamental to certain religious doctrines. In business the well-known fact can also be fundamental to a doctrine and serious mistakes can be made as a result. Money was wasted by a company that employed an army of auditors and stock takers simply because a rather paranoid management were quite certain that unless regular checks were made the employees would steal everything in sight. As in any business there was a certain amount of loss by theft, but when it was suggested that the checking could be reduced to save money it was argued that the risk was too great. This argument was founded on nothing more substantial than a form of company folklore — the well-known fact that the employees were a collection of thieves. Strangely no one queried the recruitment system which could result in such a situation!

Another 'well-known fact' trotted out by politicians, union bosses and others is that introducing robots into industry has caused the loss of thousands of jobs and contributed to rising unemployment. The facts, as reported in the survey *Robots in British Industry* published by the Policy Studies Institute in 1986, are that in the whole of British industry robots have directly displaced only a few hundred people from their jobs. The report, based on information from 700 firms using robots, also make it clear that there is very little worker opposition to the introduction of robots — perhaps partly due to the one in twelve firms who reported that they had *increased* their staff as a result of using robots. This latter finding kills off another well-known fact that the entire British workforce is sullenly watching the robots arrive and praying for a leader to take them to the barricades in protest.

The temptation to delay

In the previous chapter the dangers of pseudo-delegation were mentioned. Pseudo-delegation is an escape route for the manager who does not want to face a decision. This form of buck-passing can also delay the decision but this is not its primary purpose. Delaying the decision is an art in itself and an ever-present temptation in a difficult situation. It is also different from doing nothing in that delaying tactics require action — often dressed up to look like positive action — to deal with the problem. The purpose is to avoid facing the decision.

In addition to referring the matter to an outsider or to a committee as adopted by the pseudo-delegator there is a whole range of delaying tactics to be avoided by the professional manager:

1   Finding that a senior executive is on a trip overseas (or otherwise unavailable) and deciding that the decision cannot be made without him. It may be quite right to wait for the senior executive to return but it is important to be sure that this is the case. It is not a healthy sign to find a company dependent on the presence of one man and if it is, the man should not be allowed to travel!

2   Arguing that it would be wise to wait for the outcome of the forthcoming election, the finance bill, the discussions on bank rates, the next OPEC meeting or next year's wage negotiations. It could be sensible to hold up a decision for one or more reasons but it is only too easy to trot something out as an excuse. The questions must be posed, 'What difference will it make to wait?' and 'Is there anything which is likely to arise from the future event which will significantly alter our position?'

3   Waiting to see what the competition do. This can be a shrewd move in certain cases when a decision has been taken. Alternative courses of action are worked out to counteract firmly the anticipated but as yet uncon-firmed action by a competitor. Otherwise, waiting to see what someone else does means abandoning the initiative to them.

The right environment

The environment within which the individual works can influence his attitude to risk and decision taking. Management has a role in achieving the most favourable environment, which is examined in Chapter 8. The nature of the business required to encourage objective thinking is outlined in a paper entitled *Managing for Recovery* prepared for Management Research Group (British Institute of Management). This paper sets out the findings of the group concerning the attributes of businessmen which encourage dynamic as opposed to static management. It is not unreasonable to conclude that dynamic management and a successful business are signs that the human factors have been adequately controlled.

These are some of the conditions, recommended in the paper, which management should aim for to encourage objective thinking:

1   An aim of achieving growth and an increased market share.
2   Provision of finance to meet business needs.
3   Long-term planning and objectives.
4   Expectation and recognition of performance and rewards for it.
5   An active board of directors with non-executive members and a chairman who is not the chief executive.
6   Training and retraining of employees to meet changing needs.
7   Removal of status differences.
8   Open, relevant and easy communication.
9   Marketing and other objectives communicated to all levels.
10   Achievements communicated to all levels.
11   The human implications of change understood and given full consideration.
12   Participative decision-taking and avoidance of hierarchical barriers.
13   Ready acceptance of new technology and exploration of its possible applications.

The introduction of these conditions will not of course alter the basic intellectual or character obstacles to dealing with risk which are inherent to any individual. They might well however, modify or moderate any damaging effect and encourage creativity. For the individual there is an acid test which can assist in encouraging objective thinking. The test is to ask the question, 'If I owned the business what would I do?'

Tail piece

It seems that personal attitudes to risk taking are influenced not only by the company environment but by national cultures as well. Under the heading 'Britons take fewer risks' a UK newspaper reported the results of a study carried out for the British Venture Capital Association. The study indicated that American executives were more willing to become entrepreneurs than their British counterparts, partly because the British avoid risks. British executives were shown to be less willing to risk their pensions and have a greater fear of not getting their jobs back if the private venture fails. It was further reported that running your own business is highly regarded in the United States while in Britain only 13% of people put the owner-manager in the top status slot.

Summary

1   The personal characteristics and emotions of the individual can influence risk and decision taking. Some forms of professional training will create an in-built bias towards caution.
2   A variety of attitudes and emotions ranging from complacency to greed must be guarded against as they can result in the wrong decision being taken or no decision being taken at all.
3   Individuals must endeavour to be aware of the irrational influences in both themselves and colleagues, and management must create an atmosphere which encourages objective thinking.

4   Managements can create an environment which encour-
     ages positive attitudes and keeps the damaging human
     element under control.

Chapter 7

Help from risk-reducing measures

In addition to the ways of identifying risk, assessing it and reaching a decision, there are a number of broad actions which a business can take to reduce it. These are measures which can be built into the company operating plans to provide on-going protection and to reduce the vulnerability of the business regardless of any agonizing individual decisions which must be made from time to time.

Some risk-reducing measures relate to specific situations such as a takeover bid or a computer installation and a selection of these situations and the measures to be taken are described in the final part of this book. In this chapter broader measures are described which can be applied to a variety of situations where benefit can be obtained from risk sharing, diversification and contingency planning — or a combination of these actions.

Risk sharing by using insurance

From the earliest days of insurance and until quite recently there has existed, in one form or another, a pure system of insurance where a number of people, each in business on their own account, shared each other's risks. An agreement made between them provided for each one to contribute an agreed sum of money to compensate any one of their number for losses which he may suffer. Over the years variations on this theme have been developed, including the modern Mutual Association (described later in this chapter) and the better known market, comprising Lloyd's and the various insurance companies throughout the world. The principle of sharing the risk is still present in that although the insured business, by paying a premium, may pass *all* the risk to insurers these insurers will in turn spread the risk among themselves. Where the potential losses are high these primary insurers will take out reinsurance to spread the risk further. The insurance of expensive assets, say a fleet of aircraft, will be shared out among perhaps twenty primary insurers, each of whom further share their proportion of the cover with reinsurers, often on a worldwide basis. The business taking out insurance cover can be said to share the risk by paying a premium which, if no claims are made, is in effect a loss to the business. In addition the business may insure on the basis of retaining an excess or deductible such that it bears a slice of each loss itself.

Businesses seeking to share their risks by using insurance face a wide choice of options and at least the basics should be understood if the best arrangement is to be made. Insurance is a large subject requiring a whole range of books adequately to explain it. These comments are intended simply to draw attention to some of the more important aspects. Companies who employ an experienced risk manager can expect him or her to deal with the company's insurance matters in a professional way. Those who do not will probably arrange their insurances through a broker. This is where the problems can begin.

Choosing a broker

It should be remembered that insurance brokers are in business to make money. They do so by collecting a commission from the insurer. Thus, although in theory the broker is working on behalf of his client he is paid by the insurer, thereby creating a conflict of interest. The conflict becomes a problem when the broker has to decide between an insurer offering the best deal for you, his client, and the insurer who will pay the most commission to him. The client company can, as a result, accept a strong recommendation from a broker for a particular policy offered by a particular insurer when in fact it is the best one for the broker, not the client. The commission paid to the broker is simply added to the premium by the insurer, so the company being insured pays for it in the end and may not be getting the best value for money.

Such a situation was typified by the broker who arranged with insurers in a specialized field that he would bring them *all* the appropriate business from his clients in exchange for a commission of 15% as opposed to the 10% which other insurers in the market were offering. The deal was agreed, resulting in more business for the insurers, more profit for the broker, and higher premiums for the broker's clients — whether or not more suitable cover could have been obtained elsewhere.

The first lesson is therefore to insist that your broker obtains alternative quotations. Don't accept at face value his insistence that what he is offering you is either the cheapest cover or the best value for money. The next precaution to take is to ensure that your broker fully understands your business and properly represents the risks involved to insurers. Brokers can and sometimes do fail badly in this respect, giving unnecessarily high premiums or inadequate cover. Insist on seeing a draft of the proposed policy as a matter of routine, and check it thoroughly to see that it truly meets your needs. If, as often happens, the broker offers you a cover note and promises to send you the full documentation later, resist very strongly. The full policy documentation is a crucial part of the contract you have entered into and, if you cannot see it, you are signing blind.

When you receive the documentation you may find it full of archaic and confusing wording. You may find important clauses left out such as the clause you particularly wanted for your satellite warehouse in Slough or for storage of petrol on the premises. You may also find exclusion clauses which will reduce the value of your cover — as happened to a company insuring its physical assets. Many of this company's assets were located overseas, but in the small print was a clause limiting cover to the United Kingdom only. It is the broker's job to see that these things do not happen. Go through the wording line by line with him insisting on an explanation of any confusing wording. Check that you are getting what you are paying for.

If you do not obtain full satisfaction try another broker. It is in any case, a good idea to employ two or more brokers as this keeps them on their toes. Brokers also tend to specialize and if your business is large and varied in its nature you may need a range of insurance skills to deal with your requirements.

Deductibles and limits

The deductible or excess is the amount of each claim that the insured undertakes to pay himself. In other words a deductible of £1,000 means that the insurer will pay only £9,000 of a £10,000 loss. Premiums should be adjusted downwards for the company which opts for a higher deductible since in effect the insurers are taking less of the risk.

At the other end of the scale is the limit, the maximum amount that the insurer will pay in the event of a claim. Thus, if an aircraft is worth £10 million but the limit of cover is £5 million pounds then a total loss will result in a payment of only £5 million, leaving the aircraft owner to carry the rest of the burden himself. It is clearly important to reach the right decision on levels of deductible and limit. Some insurers will give you no choice but you should always try to get one.

Many businesses find it hard to decide which deductible and limit to choose. The question is a difficult one, but the following formulae may help. If the premium is reduced as a result of having a deductible choose one at the highest level which will not seriously damage the business, taking into account the value of the premium reduction.

If a scenario is worked out for the worst imaginable

disaster a pointer to the limit can be obtained. Suppose for example that a fleet of oil tanker lorries is being insured. The worst scenario might involve the loss of a tanker in a collision, the death of a driver or third parties, loss of the oil carried or pollution of a nearby river. A costing of all these losses will give an idea of the limit necessary to shift all the risk to an insurer. Note, however, that care must be taken to ensure that the limits discussed with brokers or insurer are 'per incident' and not 'in aggregate'. Limits are quoted both ways. Per incident means that payment for accepted claims will be met as many times as incidents occur. Limits expressed as 'in aggregate' mean that the total accumulated claims paid must not, during the policy year, exceed the amount stated.

A sad case arose with a small trading company which had liability cover to a limit of £40,000. Not only was this an unrealistically low limit for the business concerned, but since it was in aggregate it was all the cover the business would get regardless of the number of acceptable claims. When having already been paid for claims totalling about £25,000 the business found that it was only partially covered for a further loss of about £30,000, it came close to bankruptcy. The proprietors bitterly complained that their broker had not pointed out all the facts. They had been charged a low premium and their delight at this caused them to overlook the question, 'Why is this so cheap?' Naturally per incident cover is more costly as the insurer is taking a much greater share of the risk.

Deciding on the risks to be covered

Some risks such as fire, employer's liability and public liability are either obvious candidates for insurance cover or there is a legal obligation to insure. It is more difficult to decide whether it is necessary to take out say, contingency cover against a customer's failure to insure goods you are leasing to him, pollution cover, kidnap cover or computer fraud cover. Unfortunately, there is no standard answer to such questions since the significance of these risks varies widely from company to company. The practical approach is to prepare

95

a list of all the possible losses which might be insured against and consider, possibly with legal advice, which of them pose a real threat to the business. The following is a checklist of some of the possibilities which should be considered:

1   Threats to property:
        Buildings
        Fixtures and fittings
        Machinery
        Stock
        Vehicles
        Goods in trust
        Documents
        Cash and negotiable documents
     The types of threat include:
        Storms, flooding, lightning and other natural perils
        Accidental fire and explosion
        Arson, fraud, vandalism and other deliberate acts
2   Potential loss of earnings *e.g.* from strikes and from the consequences of fires, vandalism, etc.
3   Accidents and damage — both to employees and members of the public
4   Other liabilities including product liability, and liabilities to authorities
5   Pollution of air, water and land
6   Professional negligence

Within these broad categories, special insurance arrangements may be required for:

     Toxic materials
     Offshore assets
     Foods and pharmaceuticals
     Malicious damage
     Legal expenses
     Business interruption
     Patents and records

Whether or not to share such risks with insurers will depend not only on how serious the threat is perceived to be, but also on premium cost. At least one business has no insurance for legal liabilities (other than that which is legally obligatory) on the grounds that premium costs are so high that the owners of the business would prefer to take a chance. 'We cannot afford the premium,' said the managing director, 'and I would prefer to go bankrupt if a disaster occurred.' Not everyone will share this view but it is thought provoking.

Insuring your people

Quite apart from the obligatory employer's liability cover which should be arranged, there is another important side to insuring your people — or more correctly, insuring the company for the *loss* of its people. In recent years more and more attention is being paid to the fact that within any business there are certain key people upon whom the business heavily depends. This is more obvious in small companies where perhaps marketing is largely dependent on one director or the back-up technology on another. However, the same can apply in large companies where an individual senior employee or director is essential for his personal contacts or specialist financial experience. This dependency was brought home to an American company when, in the 1960s, a plane crash wiped out their entire research team at a time when technical development was crucial to the business. The company promptly brought in some sensible risk-reducing rules limiting the number and type of employees who could travel together on the same plane, train or road vehicle. Other companies, aware of such dangers and the ever-present possibility of losing a key person from resignation have carefully prepared succession and personal development plans. Training seconds in command and organizing 'management in depth' are means to guard against the dangers. However, having a fully effective stand-by specialist is expensive and, in the medium to long term difficult to maintain. Once an individual is sufficiently trained and experienced to handle a particular specialization he naturally wants to get on and do it rather than be a permanent understudy. Such people reach a point where frustration causes them to move on to fresh pastures where they can use the skills they have acquired.

To meet the problem there is a growing market offering 'key person' insurance. For an appropriate premium the business can be insured against a key person being denied them by lengthy illness or death. This type of insurance is receiving encouragement from bankers aі.d other suppliers of finance through the Business Expansion Scheme who reduce their risk of financial loss by insisting that the businesses they are backing take out key person cover.

The need for this cover is particularly marked in any business which is heavily dependent on one or two people for a particular skill. Such evidence as exists indicates that the risk of losing a key person is not something to shrug off as improbable. A broker in this field is reported as saying that statistically the risk is greater than that of a serious fire (which almost everyone insures against) and that one in four men over 45 years old will not live long enough to reach retirement age.

The mutual insurance system

The mutual form of insurance has been in existence for more than a century but until recent years was mainly limited to the shipping world. In the last century shipowners got together to cover, on a joint cooperative basis, various risks for which they could not obtain cover on the normal insurance market. The mutual system they developed has served the industry well and its flexibility to meet changing circumstances has made it one of the most successful risk-sharing methods.

In more recent years the principle of mutuality has spread (and is still spreading) to other industries including freight forwarders, ship agents, ship brokers, ship managers, ship surveyors, container fleet lessors and lessees and the owners of dockside installations. Airlines have also taken a great deal of interest in this form of insurance as a result of ever-increasing premiums and the fact that this enormous international industry has hitherto had no control whatsoever over its vital insurance needs. The extent, nature and cost of cover has been decided by the traditional insurers. The airlines, through IATA, have decided to adopt the mutual system as a means to reduce uncertainty.

The mutual system is also spreading to the professions. A number of mutual associations have been set up for lawyers, accountants and other professionals. In 1986 a mutual association was formed for bankers in the US and there are signs that other businesses and industries will take a serious interest in this type of insurance in the future.

Mutual insurance is a system which has a substantial number of advantages over the traditional market, including lower costs, greater control over the cover provided and a substantial flexibility of cover.

How does the mutual system work?

A group of organizations with similar business interests (and similar risks) join together to form a mutual association, also commonly known as a 'club'. From among the members of the club a board of directors is appointed. This board will decide the policies of the club and ensure that the insurance cover provided is continually suitable for the nature of the businesses of the members and if necessary is changed from time to time to meet changing needs.

The board of directors then appoints a firm of managers (there are a number of professional club managers in existence) who administer the club in line with the policy laid down by the board. The managers undertake a variety of tasks including:

1   Rating each member in accordance with the rules laid down by the directors, *i.e.* determining the premium to be paid by each individual member.
2   Collecting the premiums from the members and investing them. It should be noted that the proceeds of the investments are held entirely for the benefit of the members of the club and unlike the normal insurance market the proceeds are not used for the benefit of outside shareholders.
3   Examining and processing claims. This is a particularly

important activity since the managers, who are expert at claims handling, work *on behalf* of the members of the club to obtain for them the best possible results. Sometimes the claim is very clear and straightforward and the managers pay the member without delay. However, there are many cases (particularly where claims are made on businesses for alleged liabilities) where with careful handling of the situation it can be shown that the liability rests wholly or partly elsewhere and there is no valid claim on the member's business at all.

4 Organizing reinsurance. The managers, who are familiar with the reinsurance market by virtue of constant contact with it, will organize reinsurance for the club as a whole or for individual members as required. They can normally obtain reinsurance at better rates than is obtainable when insurance policies are handled individually.

5 Assisting members with legal and other problems including the vetting of contracts. This is another service element of the mutual system which is not a feature of the normal insurance market.

A number of important points are worth noting:

1 The directors (who are themselves experts in the industry concerned) will, with advice from the managers, decide the nature of cover. This gives flexibility, so that whatever changes may occur in operating circumstances, the club can adjust its cover accordingly. Members do not have to wait while the traditional market considers the position.

2 The investment earnings resulting from the premiums help to reduce costs since they contribute towards any claim payments — thus reducing future premiums.

3 The managers adopt a neutral position when examining claims, unlike the normal insurer.

4 The policy wording is in the form of a book of rules which the club issues to its members, and unlike many policies it is normally clearly worded. This clarity

100

avoids arguments over the small print. In this connection it is important to note that many clubs have what is termed a 'discretionary rule' which allows the directors to agree to pay a claim even when the particular risk has not been covered under the rules. This is to allow for the unanticipated situation which, had it been forecast, would have been included in the rules. This facility adds substantial additional security to the member.

5   The club can also provide lobbying strength, to the advantage of the members. The club managers keep a close watch on official actions and put pressure on the appropriate authorities to encourage an environment which is good for the members' businesses.

The supplementary call

There is a misunderstanding sometimes heard that the mutual form of insurance offers a danger that a supplementary call, *i.e.* an additional demand for premium will be made on club members. This is theoretically possible but in practice rarely occurs.

In the early days of clubs no one paid any premium at all and money was collected from the members only in the event that one of their number had suffered a loss. This method is no longer used and each member pays a premium (individually calculated for his own particular business) and claims are met from premiums collected. In the event that the club suffers a substantial number of claims the funds could become exhausted and it would then be necessary to ask the members for a supplementary call to meet any further claims. This would be an intolerable situation in modern times when it is necessary for budgeting and cash control purposes to be certain as to what payments for insurance a business must make, and when. For this reason a properly managed mutual will arrange adequate reinsurance to reduce the chance of a supplementary call to an absolute minimum.

It should also be noted that the club will have the power to refund money to members, and/or reduce premiums, if the funds accumulated are considered to be more than necessary to meet the known and anticipated claims. Such a refund of money is not an uncommon occurrence and is more likely in modern times than a call for more money.

In summary a mutual offers the following benefits:

1   Reduced cost.
2   A substantial degree of help and service from the managers.
3   A flexibility of cover combined with a ready willingness to pay legitimate claims.

Risk-sharing by franchising

A wide range of businesses, including fast-food catering, sock and tie retailing, car repairs and drain clearing have used franchising as a means to expand. A good business idea, tried and tested, is offered, at a price, to franchisees who operate their own segment of the business within limits laid down by the franchisor and to a greater or lesser extent controlled by him. The system enables the franchisor to expand more rapidly using the idea he has developed, by using franchisees' capital to fund expansion. Franchising at the same time enables the franchisor to share the risk of expansion with many franchisees.

The franchisee must first raise the money to buy the franchise and to equip and run his business. The franchisor is thus provided with a one-off source of income, which is then supplemented by a royalty based on the franchisee's revenue. The franchisee takes a substantial part of the financial risk. Since franchisees usually finance the purchase from bank loans, the banks also take a share of the risk.

In the United Kingdom all the major banks have set up franchise departments and these have rapidly expanded. The readiness of the banks to advance money for franchises is a measure of how they view the risk. The banks are well aware, as are the franchisors, that the franchisee is responsible for his own success or failure and has a strong motivation to succeed. An established and successful format is far more likely to be a success than one started from scratch.

The story is much the same in the USA where franchising expanded by 9.2% in 1985 alone and involves an equally wide range of products and services including petrol stations, car dealerships and drinks bottling. Banks in the USA have been less ready in the past to lend money to franchisees but there has been no shortage of other lenders, and the banks are now taking more interest in this field of business.

Franchising is not, however, a route to easy money. The profits and risk sharing will depend on a carefully planned and executed programme. The first essential is that franchisees should be successful and this will depend to a great extent on the franchisor. A series of failures will damage the franchisor as well as the franchisees. In the early days some franchisors made the mistake of over-selling their schemes and entering into contracts with almost anyone who had the necessary funds. The consequence was a rash of failures as hopelessly unsuitable people tried to run their own businesses.

The franchisor must be satisfied on the following points concerning a potential franchisee:

1   The applicant has the necessary business experience (not necessarily in the franchisor's particular field) to be able to operate with a sufficient degree of commercial acumen and management skill. An applicant may be well educated and intelligent but this is not a substitute for exposure to the business world. A librarian for example who has won the pools may have the money and the education but will not necessarily succeed in the world of retail selling or in managing people.

2   The applicant is willing to be trained in the particular business concerned and is able to assimilate the training.

3   The applicant is prepared to operate the business within the format laid down and is not likely to become an embarrassing individualist.

4   The applicant can show, from his track record, an ability to work hard, accept setbacks and have the tenacity necessary for success.

5   The applicant has the right personality for the type of

business involved, *e.g.* an easy manner with customers and polite firmness with debtors.

The next step after selecting the franchisee will be to train him. The business must be available to him as a complete package including premises, standard equipment, procedures, policy, documentation, staff training manuals, supply contracts and so on. He will require training in the use of all the contents of this package but, in addition, he must have at least some ability in accounting, social skills, negotiating skills and leadership. He may additionally require a knowledge of the law relating to the business and his duties or rights under various Acts.

The training will not end with the teaching of these and other topics but will continue to the next vital element in the equation, a business plan.

The franchisor should work with the franchisee, using and reinforcing the subjects taught, to prepare a three to five-year plan setting out objectives, work to be accomplished and the associated financial picture. Having completed the plan the franchisee should have a full understanding of what he must do, how to do it *and what he should receive in return for his efforts.*

Clearly the franchisor's offer must be good value for money, giving a reasonable return on investment in two years. Unfortunately a number of franchisors have not offered value for money and have suffered the consequences in terms of reputation and long-term earnings. The wise franchisor will continue to give support after the start of the franchise in the form of advice and retraining if necessary. These precautions reduce the risk of failure of the franchisee and lead in turn to reduced risk for the franchisor.

Risk-sharing through joint ventures

Joint ventures are often used as a way to obtain the necessary resources for a major project. They also offer a means to share the risk, so that if the project is unsuccessful the participants are more likely to survive the loss. This has been recognized by governments: the Tornado fighter-bomber has parts manufactured in three different European countries. Each of the countries wanted such an aircraft. The collaboration guarantees the market size without which the aircraft would be a failure. The same situation applies in the development of civilian aircraft: Airbus Industries, despite having customers in the national airlines of West Germany, France and Spain, is seeking to widen collaboration by arranging a deal with manufacturers in the USA. It seems unlikely that without such risk-sharing partnerships Europe would have been able to develop a wide-bodied aircraft at all.

Collaboration can make possible the implementation of an otherwise impossibly expensive idea and at the same time shares the risk. Some companies, for reasons of pride, refuse to countenance the idea of collaboration with another, possibly rival, organization. This can be a short-sighted approach and needs a lot of commercial justification to sustain it.

Computing is an industry where examples of joint venture risk-sharing can be found. Sperry, the American computer company, is involved in a number of cooperative efforts. It trades in a market where IBM spends ten times as much money on research and development. Cooperative arrangements with other organizations is the way in which Sperry hopes to obtain what they call 'technology leverage' to enable them to compete with their big spending rivals.

Sperry's risk-sharing activities include:

1   Membership of the Microelectronics and Computer Technology Corporation which is made up of 21 companies (not including IBM) who have formed a consortium for joint research.
2   Collaboration with the research departments of a number of universities.
3   Joint work with Texas Instruments on large machine development.
4   Work with Hitachi on computer peripheral equipment.

Every business should seek the risk-reducing opportunities offered by joint ventures when times are hard and profit margins slender. There seems to be an opportunity for joint ventures to replace, or sit alongside, more familiar vertical integration methods of increasing profit and gaining greater control in the market place. It is expensive to acquire the downstream sales and distribution facilities for a product and equally costly to set up the upstream manufacturing resources. With the cost comes the risk. This risk can be shared by a joint venture with an upstream, downstream or even horizontally placed company. For example, a manufacturer might form a joint venture with a major wholesaler or retailer particularly where a new and promising product is in the offing. Such a move has a precedent in the financial services world where some leasing companies work closely with manufacturers to provide a 'sales aid' financing service to the advantage of manufacturers, lessor and end-user. The risk in the business is reduced by making the products easier to sell and providing more business for the lessor. The end-user in turn does not have to find the capital for new purchases.

Other possibilities include shared resources such as warehouses, container handling equipment, test laboratories, transport depots, computer services and even in-house printing services. Cost sharing of these and any other facilities results in sharing the risk.

Diversification

Various figures for the maximum 'safe' dependency of a business on a product or service have been put forward by different experts. There seems to be some agreement that if a business is dependent on one product for more than about 30% of its revenue it is pushing its luck. The failure of this product, perhaps as a result of the appearance of a more attractive substitute product, could bankrupt the company. Clearly the critical percentage will vary from business to business but there can be no doubt that over-dependency on one source of income is a dangerous position to be in. It need not be limited to products — it can also be related to customers.

In the 1960s the British subsidiary of a major American company sold about 85% of one of its main products to only

106

half a dozen customers. The loss of any one of these customers would have been critical to the profitability of the product for which a major manufacturing investment had been made. At the same time another key product was sold almost entirely to one overseas customer. This business came to a halt when for political reasons sales to the overseas customer became impossible.

This type of dependency is relatively easy to identify although, once created, is not always easy to rectify. Less easy to identify is a dependency on the overall prosperity of a large industry. The following is an example of the problems which can arise:

Lloyd's statistics of world shipping were first published in 1920 and recorded, until 1983, a steady rise in tonnage. In that year a fall (0.5%) was recorded for the first time and further falls occurred in the succeeding two years. The figures shown in the table below clearly demonstrate the substantial tonnage growth of the mid to late 1970s and the rapid deterioration of the early 1980s.

	Gross registered tons (*millions*)	% Increase (decrease)
1973	289.0	8.0
1974	311.3	7.4
1975	342.2	9.9
1976	372.0	8.7
1977	393.7	5.8
1978	406.0	3.1
1979	413.0	1.7
1980	419.9	1.7
1981	420.8	0.2
1982	424.7	0.9
1983	422.6	(0.5)
1984	418.7	(0.9)
1985	416.3	(0.5)
1986	404.9	(2.7)

Much of the reduction of tonnage is accounted for by a fall in bulk oil traffic and consequent laying-up of many of the supertankers. There was also a decrease in the number of many other types of ship with only some specialized areas such as custom-built container vessels showing any increase.

Clearly the shipowners were facing a recession in world trade and a number of famous lines went out of business or have substantially reduced their activities in the 1980s. Less obvious to the outside world is the effect on the many businesses who depend on the level of ship movements and activity in the shipping world in general. These businesses include ship brokers, ship agents, surveyors, stevedoring companies, repair yards, fuel suppliers and so on. Such businesses have suffered reduced revenues resulting from fierce competition in a shrinking market. Some have tried to remedy the situation by diversifying into other activities but have made the mistake of moving into activities which are also affected by the shipping slump.

Many ship agents, who provide services such as arranging for tugs, stevedores, chandlery and security services have set up their own subsidiary companies to provide these services. Some have also moved into ship broking and some ship brokers have developed ship agency activities. For some companies the result has been a short-term improvement in revenues but this has come about from a reallocation of the revenue available and not from an increase in the total. With deepening of the recession the short-term improvements have, in many cases, disappeared, and so have many ship agents. The west coast of America has been particularly affected and with a significant fall in traffic to the Far East a number of agents have gone out of business.

These companies followed a 'golden rule' that when diversifying it is essential to move into activities which are familiar. Perhaps the rule should be, 'Move into activities which are familiar but not if they are also affected by the problem which caused you to want to diversify in the first place.' In fact it can make a lot of sense to move into an area which is *not* familiar if the proper precautions are taken. If the necessary know-how can be acquired to operate in the new field and particularly if existing contacts or facilities can be profitably used then it may be a very successful operation. Such a move is certainly a better bet than struggling on with a dying product or service, possibly in a dying industry.

Boots the chemist offers an interesting example of moving into an unfamiliar field. In late 1986 this company set up their first Children's World shops. Although well versed in retailing, the company recognized that children's clothing, toys and nursery furniture was an area of business requiring expertise they did not possess. The solution to the problem was to recruit purchasing and management staff from companies already established in the market such as Mothercare, British Home Stores and Debenhams. Whether or not this precaution has been successful will be seen during the later 1980s and early 1990s — unless of course the already established competition is too much for them for reasons of price, product design or other counter-attractions.

It is also interesting to note that Boots is sharing the risk in this venture by setting up the first branches as shops within shops. Concessionaires taking space include clothing and shoe retailers specializing in the children's market. In this way costs are spread and the range of products on sale is increased, thereby increasing the attraction of the shops as a whole. This illustrates the idea of diversification to reduce risk and reducing the risks in the diversification itself by acquiring the necessary know-how and spreading the cost by collaboration. Boots was not, of course, reacting to a dying product or industry, but there is an example of such a situation to be found in the UK zinc die-casting industry.

Traditionally die-cast zinc products have been made for applications where low tolerances are acceptable such as toys, domestic hardware and builders' materials. The search for lighter weight and cheaper materials has replaced zinc by plastics and aluminium, with the result that many of the less alert die-casting companies have gone out of business. Others have taken up new technology enabling zinc to be cast to much more demanding tolerances and selling their products to the electronics industry. Although still based on zinc and die-casting, new products have been developed and sold to a different market. Much of this change has gone on alongside the diminished traditional applications, resulting in a maintenance of revenues (the new products are of higher value). Such carefully planned and executed diversification can reduce dependency (and hence reduce risk) *and* create opportunity.

Contingency planning

A company was moving its finance division from the City of London to a country town. The computer, on which the company depended for almost all its accounting activities, was included in the move. Careful arrangements had been made for the transfer and the new offices, including a computer room, were ready and waiting. Staff moves had been scheduled and detailed plans worked out. A final pre-move check was being carried out when the financial controller asked the team, 'What happens if the computer falls off the back of the lorry?' There was a lengthy silence as everyone contemplated the terrifying result of such a catastrophe, including an inability to prepare debit notes on which cash flow was heavily dependent. The fact was that no one had allowed for such an event or the possibility that some other event could put the vital computer service out of action. Arrangements were promptly made with a computer bureau to be on 'stand-by' in the event of any problem and as an additional precaution a deal was made with another company having a compatible machine to provide support.

In the event the computer did not fall off the lorry but, although safely installed, it did not work! The supplier's engineers needed some days to sort out the problems during which the bureau service was used to keep production going. Had the financial controller not asked his question and if no contingency plans had been made the position would have been serious.

This example illustrates the benefits of asking the 'What if?' type of question in respect to critical matters and preparing a contingency plan to deal with failure.

There are probably far too many possible danger areas for a business to cover them all. The adverse results of fire, tempest, flood and political actions alone are virtually endless. However, concentrating on the major risks narrows the field and a series of contingency plans can be drawn up under the main headings. A series of 'What if?' questions can be asked in relation to production, marketing, administration and say, research and development. Within these categories sub-headings of vital matters such as costs, suppliers, distribution, power supply or competitors' actions can be examined.

Having a contingency plan ready (and carefully thought out) is a guard against the risk of a disaster and is also a means to react positively and quickly when the blow falls — thus avoiding the damaging loss of time when everyone is rushing about in a panic asking what should be done.

A useful by-product of the 'What if?' question can be the identification of ways and means to reduce the risk of continuing problems — with or without a contingency plan. For example, if profits fluctuate to an uncomfortable degree from season to season a countercyclical product or market might be sought. Purchasing risks might be reduced by finding substitute products or negotiating penalty clauses in the supply contract. In other words wherever there is an area of worrying uncertainty something can be done.

A classic failure to prepare a contingency plan can be found in the demise of Laker Airways. Laker would no doubt point to a number of causes for the failure of his airline but one of the major elements in his problem was a fall in the value of the pound against the dollar.

Laker purchased two A-300 airbuses resulting in a dollar debit to be repaid from revenue substantially of the sterling variety. When the pound fell 26% against the dollar Laker was suddenly short of $50 million and unable to meet his debts. It is conceivable that if he had asked the question, 'What happens if the sterling/dollar ratio goes against me?' he might have reduced the risk by the use of currency options and financial futures.

Summary

1   There are some basic risk-reducing measures which can be applied generally in all businesses in addition to specific measures required for specific situations.

2   Risk can be shared by means of insurance. There are

ways to do this effectively based on awareness of the real needs of the business and the type of insurance cover which is appropriate.

3   Franchising is a means to share risk. Success depends heavily on efficient selection, training and support of franchisees.

4   A third way to share risk is by means of a joint venture. Financial risk is spread while know-how and resources can be pooled to reduce costs.

5   Diversification can be used to reduce dependency on a product or market. Avoid the pitfall of diversifying within an area of business which is threatened as a whole.

6   The valuable 'What if?' question can be posed with respect to a wide range of critical activities and situations and lead to contingency plans to meet potentially damaging events.

Part IV

Preparing for
Risk-Taking

Chapter 8

Building a sound launch pad

Top management has a *continuous* responsibility for risk. This responsibility exists whether or not some innovation is being considered or a threat to the business is evident. It is not sufficient for the management of a business suddenly to wake up and respond to an opportunity or threat when it arises — the groundwork must be ready-prepared. In other words the business must be prepared to respond effectively at short notice to situations arising and to be able to do so depends upon top management having taken the action to develop and maintain a sound 'launch pad'. These actions, added together, further reduce risk but in a less obvious way than the measures described in the previous chapter. They are nevertheless effective and necessary.

Formulating a clear strategic policy

A decision *may* be taken to make no changes in product, markets, size or structure, but such a decision is unwise in a changing world. More likely, management will recognize the need for change and work out a policy which will govern future decisions.

115

This policy should include:

1   Attitudes to new markets, *e.g.* are there any geographical areas which are regarded as attractive, or alternatively, dangerous?
2   Attitudes to the development of existing and new products. Will the application of new technology be actively sought and will this be on a continuous basis? Should the company plan say, to develop a new product each year or update existing products on a regular basis?
3   Attitudes to diversification. Is the business too dependent on one or more products or one or more markets? Will the company actively seek new sources of revenue? Are there any limitations on diversification and preferred areas of business?
4   The limits on resources the company is willing to invest in innovation. Will a proportion of the company's resources be set aside as a routine part of the annual budget for research and development? How much? Will money be made available to exploit ad hoc opportunities and to what extent?

In short, management must clarify its degree of commitment to future change and decide the limits to such change. Without this clarification the company will not be in a position to react quickly to opportunities simply because the board will spend far too long in deciding what it wants to do.

Opportunities

Time can be saved and uncertainty reduced by deciding in advance the policy and procedure to be adopted for the various *types* of opportunity which may arise. Drucker, in *Managing for Results*, points to three categories of opportunity, namely, additive, complementary and breakthrough. Additive opportunities are those involving the more effective use of existing resources such as reallocation of sales areas or factory floor layout changes. These opportunities carry relatively little risk.

Complementary opportunities are those which will

increase the size or scope of the business, such as vertical integration, a new manufacturing facility or moving into exporting for the first time. These opportunities will carry a considerable risk.

The third category, breakthrough, are those opportunities such as a new, entirely unique and revolutionary product. Breakthrough opportunities represent very substantial risks as by definition they will be of a pioneering nature.

Since additive opportunities involve little risk and are often of a routine nature decisions concerning them are often, and sensibly, delegated to divisional or departmental level. There are however some companies with highly centralized and usually inefficient decision-taking arrangements which do not do so. Such managements are often so obsessed with cost that they are unlikely to do more than think briefly about the complementary and breakthrough opportunities. They could however begin constructing their launch pad by delegating the low-risk additive opportunities to the operating level concerned. Having seen that such delegation, properly carried out, is successful, these more nervous managements may develop the confidence to take more dramatic steps.

Complementary opportunities could bring about significant change in the business and the real breakthrough could change it beyond recognition. A clear policy is required for dealing with these categories including:

1   Some ground rules as to who will make the decision.
2   How large the minimum potential return should be if the breakthrough opportunity is to be tackled. This is to ensure that a breakthrough which is technologically enticing also has real commercial rewards attached. In no case should the opportunity be taken up if the potential cost of failure would cripple the business, unless the cost of not taking it up is just as great or greater.
3   Procedures for fact-finding, analysis and finance. In other words, when the opportunity presents itself the people and procedures for dealing with it will already be agreed and understood. Responsibility will be allocated in advance to individuals and teams who will know what is expected of them.

117

Setting up an organizational framework which allows for change

Successful development requires a high degree of coordination of the functions involved. Any failure of understanding or communication between marketing, design, production, finance and administration can result in waste of time and money (at best) or total inability to deal with the problem (at worst). The organizational structure must at least permit and preferably actively encourage, the necessary coordinated action.

It is equally important to create within the company framework a clearly identifiable department or division, with well-defined responsibility and authority for innovative action. This function can include the monitoring of the market and, especially important, close liaison with customers using the company products. Not only will a close link with customers provide prior warning of the need for product development but will also provide ideas for new products. A good example of this can be seen in IBM which, by working closely with its customers, has been able to find and develop customers' ideas in the use of computer hardware and software. Clearly less risk is involved in developing an idea which one or more customers have found to be useful.

Most importantly, sufficient flexibility must be maintained in the organizational structure to move people around to create project teams from a number of departments and disciplines. Project team members should, for example, report to the team leader and not be obliged to take instructions (or give reports to) the managers of the departments they come from.

Ensuring adequate motivation

A well motivated team — not discouraged by fear of failure and threats of punishment — is a must. At critical times in the innovation process teams and individuals may be called upon to accomplish 'impossible' tasks, work through weekends and scrap work done and start again when things go wrong. The necessary degree of motivation and enthusiasm cannot be gained by threats or the use of traditional salary scales and rewards for long service. An active and creative environment will be encouraged by:

- A high standard of working conditions
- Freedom to use initiative and to innovate
- Recognition of good work
- Tolerance of mistakes
- Flexible salary awards
- Top management support and encouragement
- Adequate financing
- Adequate training

A technique which has succeeded in practice is to take the originator of a good idea out of his normal job and to provide him with the time and resources to develop his idea. Almost everyone responds with increased energy and enthusiasm when given the chance to make their own idea work.

Ensuring that the right know-how exists

The skills required for a development project include:

- Project management
- Market research
- Marketing
- Publicity and public relations
- Financial planning
- Legal research
- Purchasing

Management must ensure that the skills likely to be needed will be available when needed. This requires a training and development programme possibly combined with an up-to-date knowledge of where specialized skills can be acquired outside the company — and at what cost.

If it is intended that individuals will be moved to staff a

119

project team, provision must be made for succession so that the individuals concerned can be released from their normal jobs.

These four functions of top management will substantially reduce the risk in taking on a new opportunity or responding to a threat. Should any of the four functions be neglected delays will occur, work will be of inadequate quality and resources will be wasted.

The creative atmosphere

A less tangible but equally important part of the sound launch pad is a creative atmosphere throughout the business. This is not easy to achieve, especially if the business is run by people who are not entrepreneurial. Responsibility for creating a dynamic environment will depend on the chief executive and his immediate colleagues whose job it is to see that the human reaction obstacles to risk taking (as described in Chapter 6) are removed.

An autocratic, oppressive style of management which devotes time to investigating failure places the fear obstacle in the way of entrepreneurial thinking. Dedicated mediocrity is the only type of work which survives in this atmosphere. People who flourish here are entirely unsuitable for taking or handling risk.

Mediocrity in management is self-sustaining since it repels the more energetic and able people, who cannot find job satisfaction. One practical way to build a thrusting but controlled environment is to create a business development team. The existence of such a team will demonstrate the support of top management for entrepreneurial action. Attitudes to risk will gradually change as a result. At the same time a carefully selected, properly used team can be a highly effective means to reduce risk by virtue of its effectiveness in action.

Using a business development team

The team must be made up of imaginative and experienced people. It must be given freedom to act within the parameters of company policy. The team members will need to have had first-hand experience of the main operations of the company and be familiar with its products, markets, finances and systems. The team leader should be a generalist not a specialist, to avoid too narrow an outlook.

It should be expected, however, that a *new* team will have a great deal to learn and one of its primary objectives will be to acquire familiarity with a wide range of subjects and to develop skills in several. Possession of this know-how is one of the major advantages of a development team which, after a time, will be able to bring a number of skills to bear on new problems. The range of skills can include:

- Project planning and control
- Questionnaire and interviewing techniques
- Analytical techniques including statistical methods and costing
- Sources of information and how to use them
- Product design
- Insurance
- Computer applications
- Sales techniques
- Press relations

Other benefits which a permanent team can provide are:

1   Developed and maintained personal contacts in government departments, banks, press agencies, advertising agencies and all the other external bodies whose help may be needed.
2   In cases where a new venture is being launched the team can provide a 'turnkey' operation. In other words the team will follow the project through from the initial idea to fruition and hand over a going concern to a management team. The hand-over can be eased if one of the team members acts as boss of the new operation for the first few months and trains his successor. It is important however that a firm deadline date for hand-over is agreed and adhered to, otherwise the develop-

121

ment team will be eroded away by losing its people into line management.

3 The team, being exposed to the outside as well as inside world is well placed to assist with corporate planning. Its experience in researching and making contacts outside the company will give it an insight into industry trends, which can be helpful in ensuring realism in the corporate plan. The team will also be better placed to ensure that any proposed innovation fits comfortably with long-term strategy.

4 The existence of the team avoids the need to pull people 'out of line' to deal with a problem or opportunity.

5 The team will have time and resources to devote to matters which otherwise are frequently added to the chief executive's workload. The team will reduce the dependency on one man to get results.

6 The work of the team, within policies designed to encourage change, takes place in a managed and controlled way, thus minimizing risk.

7 The existence of the team places greater priority on new business activity — a subject which will inevitably be competing with routine work if it is the part-time responsibility of line management.

Smaller companies may feel that a permanent team is too expensive to justify and this may indeed be the case, particularly where the need for change is infrequent. A cheaper alternative is to have one executive 'on call' as a problem handler. Such a person will need a good understudy who can take over from him at short notice and he will need time for training in the skills he may need to exercise from time to time. He may also need to maintain contact with outside specialists (*e.g.* marketing or financial consultants) who can be called in as needed.

Experience has shown that the development team should be an autonomous unit reporting directly to top management. If, as sometimes happens, the team is part of the marketing department, work on new opportunities and problems will conflict with the day-to-day demands of more routine work.

Development work must be allowed to go on uninterrupted if any real success is to be achieved.

The job description of a development team will vary from one business to another depending on the size of the organization, the long-term corporate plans and other factors. However, the following duties are suggested:

1 Monitoring the progress of company products and services, market trends and competitors' actions to spot opportunities and threats.

2 Reporting opportunities and threats to management with proposals for action which have been checked for suitability and feasibility.

3 Examining new ideas and, if appropriate, developing them to implementation. Such ideas may emanate from other people within the business. The development team must avoid 'pinching' the idea and any subsequent credit for it. Full recognition must be given to the originators of ideas who should at least be given the opportunity to know what the team is doing. Better still, the originator of the idea will work with the team, or in it, during the development stage.

4 Seeking ideas from outside the company, evaluating them and developing those that are beneficial and acceptable to management.

5 Monitoring and evaluating technological advances and, where appropriate, introducing them into the business.

Some of the most successful development teams also provide a trouble-shooting service to divisions of the business. Care must be taken, however, that the team does not deteriorate into a 'dirty job squad' which takes on the tasks which line management should deal with but prefers to avoid.

The old training problem

Training appears as a topic in almost every management textbook. Although most managers agree it is important many ignore it and almost all are bored by it. The result is that training is too often neglected, and this can cause failures when vital innovation is implemented. The introduction of new technology affords many examples of costly failure resulting from insufficient attention being paid to training. In a report published in 1986 by Strathclyde University, *The Effect of New Technology on Work*, poor training was cited as one of the major problems when new technology was introduced. Training was found to be regarded as an unwelcome expense.

A sound launch pad will include a budget and an enthusiasm for training. Committing people to a new business activity without teaching them how to do it is about as sensible as pushing soldiers into battle without teaching them to shoot. The result will be the same in both cases unless costly reinforcements are rushed in at an early stage.

The old communication problem

Everyone agrees communication is important, but most managers do little to encourage it. Gestures, such as a few words from the chairman in the company newsletter, are not enough when important changes are planned — it really *is* important to communicate the facts to the employees.

New working methods, new products, takeovers and additional premises are of great interest to the people in a business. Good communications are not only a recognition of the needs and feelings of employees — they are a fundamental part of reducing risk. Well informed people will:

1   Act more intelligently. If something goes wrong the significance of the problem will be more readily seen and dealt with.
2   Be more enthusiastic about the project. Ill-informed people spread rumours which are invariably damaging. Information removes fears.
3   Provide valuable information from the shop floor or market place to the management.

Manager/worker communication often breaks down when an intermediate stage is introduced. Passing information to the work force via union officials, working parties or the chairman's personal assistant is likely to delay or distort it. Managers must explain things directly — which means actually going to the shop floor, the market place and the offices.

Good communication should:

1   Treat people as intelligent. The average IQ is the same at all levels in a business. Waffle and half-truths are rapidly recognized.
2   Avoid unnecessary secrecy.
3   Give people the opportunity to ask questions. This helps to ensure their full understanding and indicates where the message has been badly expressed.
4   Provide the opportunity for feedback — good communication is a two-way process.
5   Not rely on announcements on the company notice board.
6   Be prompt — otherwise the information will leak out in a distorted form.

Ideally the launch pad will include communication training for managers and provide for communication in any project plans. Remember too that the outside world may be interested in what is going on and something should be ready for the press, customers and suppliers.

A ha'p'orth of tar

Whoever is made responsible for an innovation, whether it be a fully manned development team or one or two individuals given a temporary assignment, their work must not be impeded by a lack of basic services and support. Launching a significant innovation needs support. This is not a plea for unlimited resources but for the provision of at least the essentials in order to be able to work efficiently. Above all the team must not have their enthusiasm dampened by frustration with petty restrictions and bureaucratic regulations.

Among the requirements, apart from secretarial or typing

services, will be adequate space, communication and computer facilities, and easy access to reasonable funds for expenses.

A cautionary tale

An interesting example of a failure to achieve targets resulting, at least in part, from not getting the launch pad right can be found in the UK newspaper *Today*. This new daily was launched in the spring of 1986 with an estimated breakeven point for daily sales of 300,000 copies at 17 pence each. The initial circulation target of 700,000 copies clearly indicated a substantial profit and a figure of about £20 million (including advertising revenue) was talked about as a serious possibility.

Three months later it was clear that something was wrong. Sales were level at about 400,000 copies per day and the cover price was increased to 20 pence. At these levels a profit *should* have been made (the estimated breakeven point had been exceeded) but advertising revenue was below target and staff costs had risen sharply. The original plan allowed for about 500 employees but by the start date in March the actual number was close to 600. A month later a further 100 employees were added to the payroll and costs were rising fast.

A number of difficulties were reported, including problems with picture quality, but it is enlightening to look behind the scenes where more fundamental problems seem to have existed. When Terry Cassidy took over the running of the newspaper in July 1986, four months after the launch, he said in an interview with another newspaper that:

1   The financial controls of the paper were 'quite sketchy'.
2   His priority was to pull together a team of six to run the paper. The team would include a director responsible for all the revenue-earning departments and others to control production, finance and personnel. Only four of the six people needed were already on the staff.
3   'In-house husbandry' needed attention, including problems of production, circulation and distribution.

126

4   A professional marketing plan was needed.
5   Reducing waste could bring down the breakeven point.

In other words there were a number of shortcomings in the launch pad. This example illustrates the importance of attention to all the details. Finances must be controlled and the ways and means to do it thoroughly worked out and installed. A 'quite sketchy' arrangement will not be enough. Someone must be clearly and firmly in charge of each main function and they in turn should have someone to report to. They will need clear and unambiguous objectives, well understood, fully communicated and backed up with monitoring systems to check progress and give early warning of any adverse trends.

To prevent waste, there must be *sensible* controls over purchasing, space allocation, secretarial expenses and other overheads.

Summary

1   Any successful innovation will depend on having a sound launch pad. The company must be geared up for change.

2   The launch pad will include policies on innovation.

3   Knowing in advance how the various types of opportunity will be dealt with is necessary to avoid delay and to act effectively.

4   The organizational framework must be geared to encourage coordinated action and clarify responsibilities.

5   Conditions of work and employment are important in achieving the necessary level of motivation which in turn is necessary for successful innovation.

6   A range of skills are needed as part of the launch pad and ensuring that they exist is part of the top management role.

7   A creative atmosphere is required. Innovation will stall if management is dedicated but mediocre. Mediocrity is also self-generating.

8   A business development team is a good, practical way to accomplish change and minimize risk. Such a team also offers other benefits including a valuable source of information for corporate planning and policy formulation.

9   Training and communication are important subjects — too often ignored in practice. Their absence or neglect increases risk.

10   Projects can be endangered by petty restrictions on expenditure or bureaucratic controls. Support must be given in the form of facilities and funds.

Chapter 9

Opportunity, ideas and plan

A report prepared in 1983 by the New Business Panel of the British Institute of Management referring to new and smaller firms, pointed out the following common shortcomings:

- The inability to pinpoint market opportunities
- The inability to assemble good ideas
- The inability to formulate viable business plans

The report stated that these and similar problems were more significant in terms of success or failure than any lack of technological or market opportunities!

These comments suggest that companies are inhibited in making progress by inherent lack of know-how and this may put them at risk. At the same time these shortcomings will make any new venture that is attempted less likely to succeed through lack of a viable plan of action. There is ample evidence from the failures of large and long-established businesses to show that these difficulties are not limited to the small, new firms and to a greater or lesser degree are present across the whole spectrum of business. Fortunately the solutions to the problems are the same for both small and large enterprises and fortunately they are relatively simple. This chapter deals with the necessary steps, each of which will be illustrated by the real-life experiences of a company which succeeded in a major venture. The name of the company and others involved have been disguised and certain circumstances altered to preserve anonymity but the work described is exactly as it happened.

Pinpointing the market opportunity

An executive working for a London-based service company (let us call them Expand Ltd) was visiting a foreign city in the course of solving a customer's problem. During various meetings he met the head of a local company (not a customer) who expressed his admiration for the way in which the executive was helping his customers. He explained that his own business used a particular service provided by another London company (Oldhand Ltd) but that he was very dissatisfied with the service and the way it was provided. He asked if there was any possibility of Expand Ltd providing an alternative.

This was reported back to Expand Ltd's head office and after some enquiry into the potential market available and the strength of the competition it was decided to carry out a study to see if there was an opportunity to be exploited. The job was passed to the development team who took the following steps:

1   After careful preparation eleven companies using the service were visited and their needs discussed in some detail, with care being taken to obtain a clear understanding of how their businesses worked and the part played in them by the service. Their reasons for any dissatisfaction were also carefully noted as were their ideas for improvement. It was found that all were dissatisfied in some significant respect and most particularly with the design of the service. There were some fundamental flaws which arose from changes in business practice which had not been allowed for since the service was first provided many years before. In other words, the service was significantly out of date.

2   A careful analysis of the dissatisfactions was made and

130

an outline of an improved service designed. The financial aspects were examined and cash flow scenarios worked out. This preliminary costing showed that a well designed rival service could be profitable.

3   The improved service was then discussed with the first eleven companies visited, a further twelve companies and the head office staff of a trade association to which many users belonged. This resulted in a number of suggestions for improvements to the first design and, encouragingly, a very positive interest in the possibility of a new supplier with a better service to offer. It was also found that whilst Oldhand Ltd was the leader in the market there were several other suppliers and that none offered an entirely satisfactory service.

4   The design was now further revised and the new version checked again with a number of key potential users. A check was also made on the legal aspects at this stage.

5   The development team now prepared a report summarizing their work and findings. The report, which included their estimate of likely costs and rewards which would result from entering the market was submitted to the board of Expand Ltd who gave their authority for the team to go ahead.

By the end of this stage (which took about six months to accomplish) the team had pinpointed the market opportunity, evaluated it and started the process of assembling ideas. Having gained company backing the next phase commenced.

Assembling good ideas

The team, taking account of everything they already knew, retired to a conference room and, well equipped with flip charts and coffee, started a brainstorming session. The rest of the day was spent in sorting out the various ideas and listing them. Among the most important conclusions to emerge were:

1   The initial stage of drawing up a plan of action would

best be handled by one man who would seek the advice of others as required.

2 Selling the new service would be more dependent on the educating of potential customers than the hard-sell approach. Brand loyalty, aversion to change and general inertia could best be overcome by explaining the advantages of the new service at seminars in selected centres around the world. The presentation would include a description and analysis of customers' needs and how the new service would meet them.

3 The shortcomings of the competitive services would not be mentioned but a clear and rational explanation of the new service would allow users to draw their own conclusions.

4 A press reaction could be expected as soon as the news leaked out. Although everything would be kept under wraps for as long as possible a statement for the press should be ready at all times in case of need. If the news did spread the press would be given full cooperation.

5 The resources of the company were too limited to offer the service on a worldwide basis from the outset and the marketing plan should include a number of country categories. The more promising countries would be in category A, the second string in category B and the relatively unattractive areas in category C. There were also some countries with which, as a matter of policy, the company would not trade at all. The sales effort would be geared according to this categorization. Seminars and other active work would be devoted to the A category while the B group would be limited to passive selling, *i.e.* an active response would be made only to a clear interest by users in the countries concerned. Category C would receive literature and Expand would respond to enquiries by letter, telex or telephone.

Armed with these ideas the team member chosen to design the action plan started work.

The plan

The planning work started with a statement of objectives along the following lines:

- To begin providing the service by (date) and, in the first month, to have finalized at least 50 contracts.

The average expected value of each contract had already been worked out so that the financial target was part of the objective.

The next step was to put together a detailed list of things to be done on the basis of the planning cycle shown in Figure 9.1.

It will be seen that in using the planning cycle the first

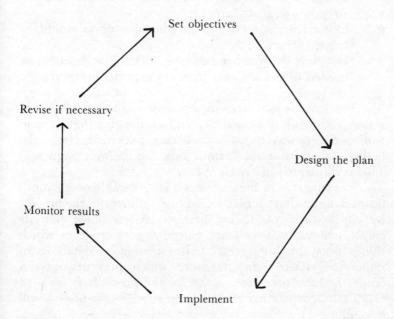

Figure 9.1 *The planning cycle*

step towards achieving the objective is the plan of action itself. This was first put together in the form of checklists of things to be done including:

- Preparation of an explanatory brochure
- Journals to be used for advertising
- Target list of 100 potential customers
- Deciding where seminars should be held and who should be invited
- Setting up and registering a subsidiary company to provide the service
- Information to be communicated internally
- Press announcements and policy
- Systems for monitoring progress
- Assistance needed from other departments
- Office procedures and computer systems
- Design of letterheads, invoices and other documents
- Accounting procedures
- Critical items for which contingency plans would be needed
- Deciding the number and type of people who would be needed to run the new business expected to result

The various jobs were than transferred to a timetable of action leading up to launch day. In fact, the plan that Expand Ltd drew up was based on working backwards from the launch date putting the various jobs into the right sequence. This is illustrated in Figure 9.2.

The diagram in Figure 9.2 is a considerable over-simplification of the chart actually used but it illustrates the process by which each job to be done is broken down into its constituent parts, which are placed in the order in which things must be completed. This attention to detail is an important risk-reducing measure which prevents, say, a failure to have brochures ready for the press. It is on such small but sensitive matters that the success of a project will depend.

The chart was further refined by allocating a period of time for each job to be completed. Target dates for completion of each stage were entered and Expand Ltd were fortunate

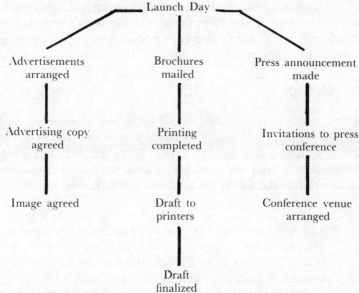

Figure 9.2 *Project flow chart*

in finding that it was feasible to do all the work in time for the launch date they had chosen. This was the most favourable date that they could find, avoiding holiday periods and taking account of the dates when the existing contracts of major target customers expired. If the work to be done had not been possible in the time available a new launch date would have been required. They had already decided that it would be unwise to put the project at risk by not allowing more than adequate time for all the preparation work to be done properly and would have postponed the launch day if necessary. As a further precaution a contingency allowance had been built into each job duration. This allowance varied from 10% to 25% according to the complexity of the job and the degree of dependence on outsiders such as printers.

The next stage of the plan was to allocate to the team members responsibility for the jobs to be done. Adding up all the man-days showed that the bulk of the work could be done by two people (one of them coordinating) with the occasional help of a number of specialists both inside and outside the company.

The team now had a clear programme of work to be done showing the deadline dates and the person responsible for each item. The only remaining requirement was to set up a system to keep track of events.

Monitoring

The coordinating member of the team was the person most concerned with monitoring progress and he decided to do this in the simplest (and cheapest) way he could find. The job to be done was not so complex that a computer would be required and the following methods were chosen:

1   A large-scale copy of the chart was pinned to the office wall where it would be visible to all the team members. This provided a constant and visible *aide mémoire* which enabled anyone to see which stage any particular item of work should have reached by any particular date.
2   Checklists of work to be done were handed to individuals. Each checklist showed only the work required of the individual receiving it but the deadline dates were clearly stated.
3   A weekly progress meeting was arranged. It was agreed that this meeting would take place *come what may*. At the progress meeting each participant would briefly report on progress and the coordinator would ensure that the effect of any delays or problems would be assessed in the light of the plan as a whole and appropriate remedial action taken. If necessary the plans would be revised (see Figure 9.1) to bring the project back on course.

This was how Expand pinpointed the opportunity, assembled their ideas and set up a plan of attack. It will be seen that a great deal of detail was considered — this being regarded as essential to reduce the risk of failure. Expand knew that in addition to the costs of the project they were exposing themselves to the possibility of a damaged reputation since they had, in the preliminary stages, contacted some important and influential companies who now expected results.

The next chapter will deal with the implementation of the project. Here we will look in more detail at some of the considerations necessary to minimize the risk of a new project.

Marketing

In launching any new project, however superior, the brand loyalty of customers to existing products can be a major obstacle. Brand loyalty is a convenient term which covers a number of underlying influences. Breaking brand loyalty is not merely a matter of saying, 'Our product is better, buy from us.'

The project plan must include positive actions carefully designed to deal with brand loyalty by tackling the underlying influences. Expand was lucky to be presented with a market exhibiting low brand loyalty which was eager for a better service. Nevertheless, Expand did put careful thought into this question, recognizing that not all potential customers would be eager for change.

The brand loyalty problem can be tackled in the following ways:

1 Present very clearly the benefits offered by the new product. These benefits must mean something to the customer and should be developed during the product design stage from information gained from the market place. Features which the supplier thinks are benefits are not good enough and the only attributes of the product which count are those which look attractive from the customer's standpoint. Peters and Waterman in *In Search of Excellence* make this comment: 'The excellent companies are better listeners. They get a benefit from market closeness.' It is therefore necessary to spell out the benefits clearly in the context of the user's needs and using his language. Once the benefits have been fully understood by the customer, his inertia will begin to weaken. Ideally the benefits will be translated into attractions for *the individual* representing the customer, as it is individuals who buy things, not companies.

137

These individuals will need inducements in the form of product/service benefits to rid them of fears of making a damaging mistake if they switch suppliers. It is the job of the salesman to deal with such situations and this is not a book on sales technique. However, the project plan must look far enough down the line to include steps to minimize the risk of the product failing simply because it is difficult to sell.

2   Complacency results from the customer feeling entirely content with things as they are and not seeing any dangers in sitting tight. This complacency must be shaken in order to get the customer to seriously consider the new product. This must not, however, be attempted by knocking the opposition. The desired result can be achieved by stressing the benefits of the product in such a way that absence of them is clearly a loss to the customer. Once again this is a part of sales technique where the losses resulting from *not* using the product are pointed out. However, the necessary benefits must be built in at the design stage and be included in the plan.

The people

During 1986 there were a number of press reports in the UK pointing out the difficulties caused in business by a shortage of skilled scientists and engineers. It is essential, as part of the project plan, to confirm what sort of people are needed, and to ensure that they will be available at or before the implementation stage. Obviously any scheme, however good, can fail to get off the ground for lack of the right people.

Coordination and cooperation

More than one carefully organized sales campaign has run into trouble through a shortage of product at the critical moment. This can be due to a failure to ensure that the manufacturing side of the business has been fully informed of the needs, because their estimates of the lead-time to full production have been ignored. In one case everything came to a grinding halt due to lack of raw materials. No one thought to involve the purchasing department until it was too late!

The plan must include a provision for coordination and cooperation (both of which require communication) to ensure that everyone is in step.

Timing

Sometimes there is a particularly good time to launch a project and often some very unfavourable times. Expand worked back from its chosen launch date and found that it could fit all the work in with a comfortable contingency allowance. Checking that the time available *does* allow enough time is at least as important as choosing the best launch date.

The competition

There is always a danger of being pipped at the post by a competitor. Avoiding this depends heavily on keeping abreast of what competitors are technically capable of and watching their activities in the market closely. Studying the competition's annual reports will give some clue as to their financial resources and capabilities — always a limiting factor to innovation.

The biggest danger lies in having an unprepared and indecisive management which is unable or unwilling to reach a quick decision. While such managements are pondering over the information presented to them a more positive competitor company will be taking action. An American civil war general is alleged to have said that the winner will be the commander who 'gets there fustest with the mostest'.

Financing the project

In an earlier chapter one of the suggestions for guidance in making a decision was calculation of the best/worst scenario. Hopefully the worst case will be calculated on a realistic basis.

In the planning stage similar realism is required in working out the financing of the project. This financing can arise from:

- Internal company funds, *i.e.* reserves or income from established products
- Self-financing from sales of the new product
- Borrowed money, *e.g.* bank loans
- A combination of any of the above

The plan must include a cash flow forecast to show the financing required and the sources of the money. When preparing this part of the plan a number of contingencies must be taken into account and sub-plans prepared to take care of them.

It must be recognized that in many cases in the past businesses have gone ahead on a project on the basis of sensible analysis only to find that in the time that has elapsed between making the decision and getting the programme under way things have changed. Similarly, the environment can change after the new product has been launched. The changes can be beneficial but they can also be damaging. New business plans dependent on the price and demand for oil are clear examples of this problem, as is witnessed by idle oil rigs, empty rig building yards and laid up tankers. At the time the rigs were ordered even the worst case scenario looked good, the yards were busy and the tankers in demand.

The risk depends to some extent on the lead-time between the decision to go ahead and the launch date of the product. The longer the time which elapses the greater the chance of an adverse change in the business environment. In recent years computer manufacturing, factory and office building, textiles, plastics and chemicals among others have experienced some catastrophic events resulting from environmental shifts. Protection depends on asking the 'What if' question and including in the plan some resulting contingency measures.

For example, what if . . .

- There is a recession and sales fall to x% of the estimated amount?

- Raw material costs rise by y% in the first two years?
- Interest rates go up by z%?

Some problems can be caused by success — for example, sales may be greater than expected and give rise to higher inventory costs. Likewise, higher sales combined with delays in collecting money from customers can cause liquidity difficulties. It is important in the financial part of the plan not to underestimate the amount of money which may be needed. If sales fall or costs rise then more funding may be needed. The plan must therefore allow for a possible need for additional financing, and thought must be given to the security that a lender will reasonably require. The lender could of course be the company itself providing money from the earnings of established products, in which case the capacity of the company to meet the need must be taken into account. Alternatively, if recourse must be made to a bank or other outside body then a sufficiently convincing case will need to be prepared for presentation to them.

Another problem to be avoided is that of putting too much of the company's financial resources into the first version of the product or service, leaving insufficient reserves to produce an improved version which market experience may show is needed to sustain sales growth. Planning to hold some reinforcements in reserve will give management some flexibility.

Controls

Some monitoring aspects of control have already been mentioned. However, those were primarily concerned with control of the development project itself. There are two other aspects to build into the plan, namely control of the business operation after launch of the product, and control of project expenditure. The project plan should include identification and description of work to be done in the management of the new product. This is particularly necessary if a new company is to be formed or acquired. If it is intended that the new product will be added to an existing range, then it is likely that the management will already be set up with the necessary procedures and administration. If, however, a new and possibly autonomous entity is to be created for the new venture, then in addition to operational questions the way in which the business as a whole is to be controlled must be worked out.

An illustration of a failure to control a new business is found in the history of Vehicle & General Insurance Company which collapsed in 1971. V & G grew rapidly from the start as a result of offering low cost motor insurance based on the concept of the 'proven motorist'. This somewhat theoretical character had a claim-free record and had thereby (it was said) proved himself as someone who was unlikely to make claims in the future. Whether or not this reasoning was right is debatable but the fact is that V & G dropped its controls and began to insure quite a lot of 'unproven motorists'. As the number of these clients grew so did the likelihood of a normal level of claims, which the premiums did not allow for. Inevitably V & G went down, leaving a lot of motorists uninsured.

The command structure of the new business and its operating standards are all part of the control process and must be worked out and agreed. The US Special Forces failed to do this in planning their attempted rescue of hostages in Iran. All three services insisted on playing a prominent role with a resulting confusion in control and command. With the added problem of faulty equipment and a weak leadership within the strike force the mission was a ghastly failure.

Expenditure on the development stage of the project itself must also be controlled despite the fact that this is normally a relatively small sum. Overruns on the development budget are likely to attract unfriendly comment from those who were lukewarm or opposed to the idea. A budget should be drawn up at the outset and performance against it monitored by the project coordinator. Each participant should take part in preparing the budget and know how much money is allocated to each activity. The monitoring should be close, but at the same time over-rigid adherence to the details of the budget should be avoided. The flexibility to switch money from one heading to another within the budget should be allowed in

142

order to take up opportunities for improvements. This flexibility must not be abused however, and should be subject to agreement at least with the project leader or, better still, with the whole project team.

Communication

Continuous communication within the project team is essential to avoid duplication, neglect and muddle. Expand used their regular weekly meetings to ensure that each member of the team knew what was going on. In addition to this intra-team communication, the team also needs to keep in regular touch with the rest of the company and the outside world. The latter can be handled using press releases, press conferences, seminars, visits to customers or suppliers and even cocktail parties for politicians and union leaders.

The type of communication will vary from project to project but the following are some of the possibilities:

1 Discussions with potential suppliers, to ensure raw materials of adequate quality, price and availability.
2 Visits to government departments, to obtain guidance on licensing requirements, to find out what support for exports may be available or to assess political attitudes.
3 Talks with potential suppliers of capital.
4 Conferences with union leaders, to ensure friendly cooperation and obtain early warning of potential difficulties.
5 Briefing of publicity agencies, to keep them abreast of developments and to encourage good and relevant ideas.

Communication with the rest of the company is needed to maintain the understanding and support of both top management and the various divisions. Keeping the project in front of top management will help to maintain their interest, assure them that the work is being done and give them the opportunity to make suggestions and give advice.

Keeping the heads of divisions or departments informed

143

will allow them to think and plan ahead *and* work together in preparing for launch day. It is clearly necessary for the sales and manufacturing departments to know what will be expected of them. It is a fatal mistake to present a *fait accompli* to these departments. They will not only understandably be annoyed but may be faced with an impossible task. Communicating with them (and obtaining their advice) is the way for the team to find out what is achievable and stimulate the interest of the people concerned.

Accounting

The new product or service will require appropriately designed accounting facilities. The plan should include provision for this, including early discussion with the accounts department. It may be that if, for example, a new subsidiary company is to be formed, a separate accounting system will be preferred. If so, the procedures must be established to meet the various needs and, if required, to be compatible with any central corporate accounts into which results must be fed for quarterly or annual consolidation.

It may be possible to use existing computer systems and thus save hardware and programming costs, but if a new computer system is required then sufficient time must be allowed to create it. New software takes time to complete and test. It is also a good idea to have a manually operated fall-back system so that the project start is not held up by any computer problems which may arise.

Dealing in a new market may require variations of the company's billing and credit control systems. Industry conventions on payment terms may be different from those to which the company is accustomed. If exporting is involved the design and wording of the invoice may require some special attention. For example, VAT may not be applicable but local law may require certain information to be present on the invoice, or that the local language be used. Failure to sort out these details could bring the new business to an expensive halt.

Training

Expand, among its checklists, included one on the number and type of people required to run the new business. This topic will lead the planner to the subject of training since this may be an essential part of providing the right *type* of people. The new product may require new expertise. Careful thought must be given to the knowledge and skills that managers may need — if only to be able to understand the customer's business and needs. Salesmen will need product knowledge in order to be able to sell effectively, and back-up departments such as accounts, warehousing, distribution and public relations may all need at least familiarization training. Should anyone whose contribution is needed not have the necessary information the success of the business could be endangered.

What if everything goes wrong?

There is always the possibility that the scheme may fail. One of the many external threats which were referred to in the introduction may wreck even the best-planned scheme. Or, there could be a fatal flaw in the planning or execution. Like every good general, the planner will prepare for the worst and have ready the ultimate in contingency plans — a line of retreat.

Once again the appropriate 'What if?' question should be answered with ideas for abandoning the project with the least possible damage. It may be possible to sell any capital equipment or use it elsewhere in the business. Contracts for the supply of raw materials or services need negotiated terms which will give the easiest possible cancellation. Normally some remedial steps of this sort can be taken. More difficult is the avoidance of adverse market or press reaction and a policy for explaining a withdrawal needs to be agreed. Sometimes necessity can be turned into a virtue and a really professional public relations bureau should be able to find an honest way to do this. There is no right answer to this problem but two things are definitely wrong — leaving customers in the lurch, and pretending there is no problem. The former will, quite rightly, never be forgiven and the latter convinces no one.

Summary

1   In order to be able to innovate successfully a business must pinpoint opportunities, put together good ideas for dealing with the opportunities and prepare detailed and comprehensive plans.

2   Pinpointing the opportunity involves getting close to the market place.

3   Assembling the ideas can involve the use of techniques such as brainstorming.

4   The planning process should start with a clear and unambiguous objective against which progress can be measured. The plan must be subject to a monitoring procedure and an opportunity for revision of the plan must be provided.

5   Checklists of all the various jobs to be done are a good starting point for the plan. These can then be translated into a timetable of action.

6   The team handling the project, or one of its members, should monitor progress against the plan and communicate progress to all team members. Team members must also be aware of their own responsibilities and how well or badly they are performing.

7   Certain topics are particularly important and these include marketing, human resources, coordination, cooperation, timing, financing and controls.

8   Attention to detail is essential in the planning stage to reduce the risk of failure. Also important is a get-out plan in case the project fails.

Part V

Implementation

Chapter 10

Making it go

When all the preparations are completed the implementation of the change must be faced. With careful planning this stage should be a smooth continuation of the work done so far. The objectives must be confirmed, after which all the constituent parts of the planning cycle — implementation, monitoring and revision — should progress smoothly.

Expand Ltd decided to form a subsidiary company (Goodplan Ltd) to implement its new project. All the necessary legal and other work required for this was completed during the preparation stage. In order to ensure an adequate knowledge of customer needs among the staff, Goodplan recruited two people from existing users of the service during the planning stage of the project. This allowed sufficient time to train the new people and to make use of their knowledge in planning the sales campaign. Goodplan's objective was to land 50 contracts *in the first month* after going live — a tough target.

The other steps taken by Goodplan are considered below:

Setting up the team

In addition to taking on two recruits (both in their thirties and thus young enough to adjust readily to their new environment) it was decided to make the project team leader the managing director of the new company for a period of not less than six and not more than twelve months. In addition, an experienced manager was transferred from another subsidiary to work with the temporary managing director, in order to take over from him when he had a firm grip of the new business. The team leader would then concentrate on sales for a few months to support the operation and then withdraw, leaving the new managing director fully in charge.

This way of working creates promotion opportunities for able people who might otherwise be frustrated. The motivating effect in this case was marked and Goodplan's managing director-elect threw himself into the battle with energy and enthusiasm.

The risk of choosing the wrong man to lead the new company was thus reduced by selecting a 'known quantity' from within the company. An outsider might have been equally good — or not — but seeing a career opportunity going to an outsider would not have been good for the morale of existing staff.

The Goodplan team at this stage comprised the following:

1   A temporary managing director with detailed knowledge of all the planning work and personal contacts established in the market.
2   A managing director-elect with proven ability and a period of time available to him to gain the knowledge necessary to run the business.
3   Two young executives with first-hand knowledge of how the potential customers worked and how they used the service.

There was, in addition, an appropriate number of secretarial and clerical staff.

The management style

Being a small team, communications within it were not difficult and *ad hoc* meetings and discussions kept everyone in touch. However, particular care was taken to see that the temporary managing director and his successor knew what each other were doing and this was achieved by putting them together in the same office. This gave them the opportunity for regular discussions and also for the passage of information or background as events took place. These small points, which could have been overlooked in the course of formal briefings, were regarded as vital in understanding the market and the product.

A further important and effective measure was to delegate as much as possible to the two executives. Whenever their training was completed on a particular job or topic and they expressed confidence to handle it they were given the freedom to go it alone. This policy was adopted in the knowledge that an occasional mistake would be made. These mistakes were expected to be more than outweighed by the motivating effect of the responsibility.

Goodplan gained an advantage over Oldhand Ltd whose staff worked in a rigidly controlled environment where they had to refer important decisions to head office. Goodplan had no separate sales force: everyone in the team was expected to prospect for business and negotiate deals. The freedom to act (within fairly wide parameters) made them effective and flexible.

Announcing the new service

A news leak prevented Goodplan from announcing its entry into the market at the time it had chosen. A keen reporter from a leading trade journal appeared at Goodplan's office one day demanding information. The managing director-elect was the only member of the management team present at the time as all his colleagues were visiting potential customers. As a result of the close communication maintained in the team he was aware of all the vital information so he was able to satisfy the reporter. In addition, he was able to implement the contingency plan for such an eventuality and issued a prepared and up-to-date press release immediately. Information was sent to an agreed list of UK and foreign journals

151

and a press conference announced. Further information was also sent to a list of target companies. The managing director, who was in America at the time, was fully informed by telex enabling him promptly to follow up the information with calls to the target companies.

Goodplan managed to turn an unfortunate mishap into an excellent opportunity. The result was a flood of enquiries and the absent team members had to hurry back to the office to deal with them. Fortunately all the necessary document-ation and procedures were prepared for dealing with enquiries and the team was able to cope.

A problem they had not allowed for was a steady stream of personal callers at the office wanting to discuss possible contracts for their own companies. To cope with this one member of the team was allocated the job of dealing with personal callers and any mail, telexes or telephone calls he could not handle were taken over by his colleagues.

This case history illustrates how important the planning and attention to detail is to reducing risk. First, the initial attention to the needs of the market and design of the service had resulted in something the market really wanted. Secondly, the contingency planning turned a potential night-mare into an advantage. Had Goodplan not been able effec-tively to respond to the press as it did there could have been some unfavourable reactions. The result in fact was a market response so good that the team could barely deal with it. The outcome was that the first month's objective was well exceeded with about 90 contracts concluded.

The intended marketing method

Notwithstanding the initial rush Goodplan went ahead with its longer term marketing plan on which, it believed, the main customer base would depend.

The planned seminars were held in the *A* category coun-tries (see Chapter 9) and the results monitored. Among the information collected as part of the monitoring system was:

1   The percentage of companies invited to attend a seminar who sent a representative.

152

2   The type of people who attended, *i.e.* senior or junior executives and from what department.
3   The questions asked and reactions to the answers given.
4   The percentage of companies, and their type, who responded immediately after the seminar, *e.g.* by asking for a private meeting to discuss their own particular interests.
5   The percentage of companies who responded later, *e.g.* by mail.
6   Any adverse comment or reaction.

This information was used to judge market reaction and to see if there were any regional differences. The response to the seminars gave an indication of whether or not this particular means of selling was a good one and it was also possible to forecast the likely response to future seminars. This, in turn, enabled Goodplan to estimate the amount of follow-up work which would be needed after a seminar, thus making sure that they did not stimulate interest that they could not follow up.

It was found that in some places a seminar resulted in early enquiries and quickly concluded business. In other places the response time was longer (up to six months or so) and in one country the response was nil after a year. Such variations were studied to see what, if any, local circumstances would explain them.

Once again, Goodplan was paying attention to market detail, and not allowing itself to risk the venture by making guesses about the way forward. The fact finding process was continuing and future activities were being planned on the basis of analysis of the information collected.

What about the competition?

Goodplan did not expect the competition, especially Oldhand, to ignore its activities. A close watch was kept for any competitor's reactions. Oldhand suffered from a substantial drawback, complacency.

The chief executive of Oldhand was not prepared to

believe that his company's market dominance could seriously be affected by a newcomer. He made the mistake of saying so publicly. Oldhand could have redesigned their product and shaken up their customer service but chose not to do so. Nor did their chief executive take any notice of warnings from his younger staff.

The lack of activity from Oldhand enabled Goodplan to continue its market penetration throughout the first year. It discovered that other, lesser, competitors were equally inactive and some had withdrawn from the market altogether. By the end of the first year Goodplan had gained more than 200 customers and was adding to them steadily. It was well on course for 300 customers and, equally important, it had captured all the major accounts.

By contrast Oldhand lost about a quarter of its customers to Goodplan, and since this included most of its major customers Oldhand's revenue fell by about a third.

Expand and their subsidiary Goodplan offer a good example of a success story based on taking care in preparation and paying attention to detail. There are, however, other requirements to be met which require explanation here.

Maintaining enthusiasm and commitment

In the early stages of any new venture doubts will surface. Those who were not wholeheartedly behind the idea in the first place will look for opportunities to spread alarm and despondency. The solution to this problem, apart from using a motivating style of management, is to review regularly progress against the plan.

If all is well and the facts, as known, still suggest the same course of action then any worry is unnecessary. This sort of reassurance must be communicated to the team from time to time, along with reassurance that if something goes wrong there will not be a witch hunt. Management can encourage commitment by making it clear that it accepts that an element of risk is inevitable.

Commitment can also be encouraged by giving tangible as well as moral support. An executive having difficulties will be motivated by practical help from his boss in the form of technical assistance, equipment or funds. Plans should allow for this. Expand made provision for various company specialists to be on call to help their subsidiary in times of need. In some situations the commitment of the people can be gained by giving them a 'piece of the action'. An example of this may be found in the experience, and success, of the British company Optare. Optare was created from Charles H. Roe Ltd, a British Leyland subsidiary which was due to close with the loss of several hundred jobs. A former senior executive of British Leyland decided to set up the new venture and he involved in it a number of former employees of Charles H. Roe. These employees contributed a minimum agreed amount of redundancy pay into the scheme and thereby had a financial incentive to see that it was a success. Two years after its launch Optare had landed impressive contracts and was expanding rapidly. Share-option schemes, profit-related bonuses and other financial incentives can help the workforce to benefit from the success of the business.

Top management involvement

Visible support from top management can be a valuable part of the start-up programme. An active interest will not only encourage the people involved but will also help overcome internal and external obstacles. A friendly word from the chairman can often influence heads of other companies, politicians or licensing authorities. Such practical help should be available from top management — but it must be given with the full knowledge and agreement of the team. Ideally, senior people will suggest ways in which they can help, leaving it to the team to take up the offer as and when required. Help should not (except in an emergency) be imposed as this smacks of interference.

Monitoring

A particularly close watch on how things are going is needed in the very early stages. Any problem which is neglected at

155

the start is liable to grow if not promptly corrected. Early feedback from the market is needed where new products are involved; the reaction of unions, employees and competitors are especially important and all available information about them should be carefully considered.

Control

At start-up, when everyone is busy, control can slip. Continual good communication is required to prevent uncontrolled activities and the team leader must double-check that everyone knows what is expected of him. Checklists and planning charts will help with progress chasing.

One example of lack of control at the start of a project involved the dumping of several hundred bags of cement on a building site. The cement should not have been delivered until a rain-proof storage facility was available and most of it was ruined in an overnight downpour. The same project later suffered from a lack of batteries required for various items of electrical equipment as a result of someone forgetting to order them.

An important aspect of control in the early stages is following up the training that was given. There may be people who did not receive adequate training and who struggle with unfamiliar paperwork, systems or equipment. Any such weak links must be quickly remedied before the project is damaged.

Some schemes are so large and complex that a special control provision will be needed. A troubleshooting squad can provide a valuable service to an inevitably busy management team. Such a squad can deal with problems seen or suspected in the market (*e.g.* by visiting retailers) or investigate, say, quality problems with suppliers. The squad can thus ensure that action is being taken on urgent matters, leaving the management team to control the project as a whole. Without a troubleshooting facility some of the problems can be neglected. The squad prevents crises from taking priority over important positive matters. It thus reduces the risk of failure.

Other possible problems which the squad can handle include:

- Difficulties with point-of-sale display material
- Misuse of the product
- Bottlenecks, *e.g.* in paperwork
- Distribution problems
- Packaging faults
- Queries from customers

Summary

1   The transition from planning and preparation into implementation of a project should be smooth.

2   The Expand example illustrates many of the essential requirements such as putting the management team in place and giving them the freedom to act effectively.

3   Publicity, either internal, external or both will be required and this needs close attention. Expand found that its careful preparations changed a potential disaster into a successful operation.

4   Marketing becomes of prime importance in the case of new products. A means to obtain and evaluate feedback from the market is vital.

5   The competition can be expected to react and their activities will require close attention.

6   Those responsible for the project may need moral or material support to maintain their enthusiasm. There is often a role for top management in this.

7   Control must be maintained. One way to make management more effective is to use a troubleshooting squad.

Chapter 11

Keeping it going

'Half the failures in life arise from pulling in one's horse as he is leaping.'
— *Guesses at Truth,* Julius & Augustus Hare

The failures which occur from time to time in business innovation have many causes, some of which lie outside the control of the innovators. Some, however, are within their control. These fall into one of three categories, the first of which is the one that the Hares had in mind.

Pulling in the horse

There is a natural tendency in some people to be frightened by success. The feeling that it is all too good to be true can cause management to have second thoughts about a new idea. One management team began to suffer from a 'Let's not go too far' syndrome as it saw a form of management by objectives (MBO) begin to stimulate the business. The scheme was working well, introducing greater dynamism in a business which had become sluggish. Seeing the increased enthusiasm of managers at all levels the board became frightened and ordered the programme to be slowed down. The task force responsible for organising the MBO scheme were bewildered,

158

and managers who had worked hard to develop lists of key tasks became disillusioned. The scheme quickly died, leaving morale low and bringing about a return to the old 'management by expediency' method which many managers had tried to eliminate.

Sometimes rising costs will deter management, particularly so when costs are more than were originally forecast. There is a trap here which management can fall into which makes failure a certainty and which is, in effect, a self-induced and unacceptable risk. Sadly managements are often led into this trap by their accountants who will draw attention to rising costs. This is the time for directors to keep their nerve and think very clearly. The scenario is illustrated by the following example:

Bloggs Engineering Ltd have developed a friction-free coating which can be used in engine bearings, pistons and a wide variety of moving parts. This invention is a great breakthrough and will revolutionize the engineering industry. Bloggs' development department is full of enthusiasm. Unfortunately Bloggs has had to spend a lot of money on research and now, just as it is about to reap the benefits, it finds that a disbelieving world wants more proof that the wonderful new coating will not break down after years of use. A major motor manufacturer and a leading aircraft manufacturer have insisted on more testing and this must be at Bloggs' expense. When the board discussed the position the chief accountant presented his cost estimates. 'We have already spent one million pounds. We will now need to raise and spend a further quarter of a million. The risk is too great,' he said.

Although the members of the board looked troubled, and were considering abandoning the project, one of the directors brought some logic into the debate. 'We have spent one million pounds and that is a fact,' he remarked, 'but it is also a fact that the money has gone forever and, if we stop now we will never get it back. The only question we must answer now is whether we want a friction-free coating, which we believe will succeed, at a cost of a further quarter of a million. If we do, let's forget the past and spend the money.'

This is the only approach which makes any sense in such situations. History cannot be rewritten and spent money cannot be recovered. Risk assessment must start by taking account of *future* opportunities and costs.

Losing interest

The second cause of failure is loss of interest. This attitude is normally a board-level problem — the people carrying out the innovation will normally be able to sustain their interest.

The problem is that once the innovation is off the ground, apart from a quarterly examination of the budget, the board tends to forget it. Often more urgent matters divert attention from the new scheme, but the fact is that the first few months of implementation of an innovation are as important as all the previous stages. Top management has three roles:

1   To demonstrate continued interest to show that they regard the work as important and, by so doing, to motivate those doing the work.
2   To uphold their duty to shareholders, who will rightly expect results from their investments.
3   To ensure that any further opportunities which the innovation may reveal are identified and properly evaluated.

This last responsibility brings us to the third cause of failure.

Not following through

Even after an innovation, management must look ahead to the next step. The most successful innovation has its own built-in mechanism for self-destruction, in that changes in the environment will inevitably render it obsolete one day. From the moment that a new scheme goes ahead the next one needs to be thought about.

Possibly one of the most outstanding examples of the *right* way to do it can be found in Jaguar Cars. By 1980 Jaguar Cars had a poor reputation for quality and reliability and sales in the important US market had fallen to about twelve cars per year per dealer. Gradually Jaguar improved the standard of their product and, at the same time, stepped up productivity at their factories. By 1985 sales per dealer in the US had risen to about 120 and productivity was about four times the 1980 figure of 1.4 cars per employee per year. By a series of innovations Jaguar had converted the XJ6 from a mediocre performer in the market into one which could not be produced fast enough to meet demand.

Not content with this Jaguar developed a new model, the XJ40, planned to go into production in 1986. This seemed surprising to many people — not least the US dealers. Tom McDonald of Jaguar US was reported as saying that the XJ6 was regarded as such a classic that dealers feared that any replacement would fall short of its reputation. Representative US dealers visited the UK in 1986 to reassure themselves that it would meet the need, such was the level of their concern.

Why then should Jaguar take what appeared to be a expensive and unnecessary gamble? The answer was given by David Boule, the public relations director, who said, 'The answer is two-fold: increased productivity and still better quality *until we are on a par with Mercedes Benz*. The XJ40 has been designed to use 1990s technology.'

Jaguar, despite having a highly successful product, looked ahead, thought about the activities of its rival and worked out what it must do to stay in a successful position. It has also set new objectives for output levels: to expand the 1986 level of production of around 42,000 cars to about 90,000 by the end of the decade.

The actions of Jaguar illustrate the need for management commitment to further development. From the start decisions must be taken on the medium- to long-term future of a new product, its replacement or its alteration. The same approach is needed to other innovations such as organizational changes, computerization, appointing sales agencies, formation of new companies or diversification.

Ideally the business will identify, as best it can, the date when a new scheme or product will approach the end of its life and initiate action for a replacement. It is important that the replacement is introduced while the first version is still successful, *i.e.* before the business is at risk.

Another example of a company which looked ahead is Optare. The product taken over by Optare was the traditional large bus, the double-decker. The chief executive of Optare was reported in the press as saying, 'We knew the bus market was going to change direction and that we wouldn't be able to trade on the back of the sort of product which had been built here previously.' Optare went ahead with nine new designs including the City Pacer built to suit the needs of bus operators experiencing a changed market. Deregulation of bus services and the economics of the market demanded a new vehicle which Optare provided. The reason for developing nine different buses also gives food for thought and was explained by Optare as aiming for a wide market, *to hedge its bets*.

Encouraging all the staff

Reference has already been made in this chapter to the need for top management to encourage those running a new scheme by taking a visible interest in it. There is also a need for those in charge to ensure that more junior employees are also given encouragement. Every clerk and typist, every fork lift truck driver and every machine operator, laboratory technician or warehouseman plays a part in achieving success for the scheme. All of these people have a natural need to know what is going on. If this need is satisfied with information they will do a better job. The information to be given depends on the nature of the job being done but graphs, charts and score boards are suggested for:

- Sales made
- Repairs completed
- Documents completed
- Product movement
- Machine output
- Down time
- Turnround times

- Customers served
- Income
- Expenditure

Knowing this information really does stimulate activity and it should be a policy of the company to provide it. Failure to tell the people down the line how they are getting on is sure to kill their interest for the simple reason that they will be working in a vacuum.

The outside world

'Nothing succeeds like success.' An old but true saying — publicizing success is another way to maintain the momentum. New customers will be attracted to a well publicized success story and detractors can be converted into supporters.

Consideration should be given to methods other than advertising as a means of publicizing success — good results can be achieved from magazine and newspaper articles. The press is always interested in such possibilities if a story is given to them.

Expand published a quarterly news bulletin for its customers which gave useful information which they had gathered from the market. This was provided on the basis that any helpful information, perhaps resulting from the experiences of a customer, should be made available to all customers. Also included was statistical evidence of the popularity of the new service and its acceptance around the world. This news bulletin was sent not only to existing customers but also to *potential* customers so that they could see the quality of Expand's service. The result was a steady stream of new customers.

Avoiding the policy obstacle

A British insurance broker, finding its overheads growing and its administrative routines in a muddle, instituted a study of all its internal procedures, and organization. A former business consultant was taken on the payroll to provide the necessary expertise. In due course plans were drawn up for dramatic structural changes, including a variety of new systems many of which were based on mechanization of slow manual operations. The preparatory work was very professionally carried out and the plans implemented smoothly. The benefits of the changes soon became apparent and the whole business became more effective. Everyone was delighted with the results in all but one area of operations — the part of the company which dealt with North American business. The consultant examined the unresolved problems in the department concerned and realized that further changes were needed in the case of work which involved a North American associate company. These were designed but, the consultant explained, could not be implemented without some work being done in the associate company. He proposed a visit to North America to do the work necessary to ensure the compatibility of the operations carried out on both sides of the Atlantic.

His employers agreed that the overseas work should be done but told him that he could not do it himself as it was company policy that only brokers could travel overseas on business! This policy, founded on the notion that the only reason for overseas travel was to obtain new business, was jealously guarded by the brokers who regarded trips to exotic places as their particular privilege. As a result of this a senior broker was given the job and the consultant told to instruct him on how to do it. The broker, having no experience whatsoever of the analytical work required and finding the instructions beyond him suggested that the consultant be allowed to go with him on the trip as an assistant! Fortunately the absurdity of the situation became apparent to all concerned and the policy was dropped to enable the consultant to do the job he was being paid for. However, this was not an easy result to achieve and many of the more senior brokers were horrified. As a consequence the arguments were lengthy and four months' precious time was lost before the job was done.

There is always the possibility that an innovation will, as it develops, be found to be in conflict with some aspect of company policy. Management must review the policy dispassionately and if necessary amend it or scrap it. The fact that a policy has been around for a long time is not in itself a reason for adhering to it and the 'We've always done it this way' attitude is dangerous. The decision should rest on which option is the least risky — sticking to the policy or changing it.

Summary

1   There is a danger of the company getting 'cold feet' around the time of the launch of an innovation. This reaction is irrational if the preparatory work has been done properly. Reviewing the facts can provide the desired reassurance.

2   Rising costs must be treated logically. Avoid the trap of obsession with past and irrecoverable expenditure.

3   Top management must maintain and demonstrate continuing interest in the scheme.

4   The momentum of innovation must be maintained. New products should be prepared when the existing ones are doing well.

5   The employees' need for information and involvement must not be neglected. Success will depend substantially on the motivation of employees at all levels.

6   Success breeds success — publicity can help. The outside world should be informed of progress — and thereby be encouraged to become customers.

7   Outdated policies may need to be scrapped or changed. Progress of a scheme must not be blocked or endangered by sticking blindly to established views.

8   Standards of control, monitoring and revision must be maintained, especially when under pressure from urgent matters. Continued attention to detail and contingency plans is needed to hold down risk.

Part VI

Some Particular Risk Situations

Takeovers and mergers

There are two sides to takeovers — attack and defence. Both sides have strong elements of risk and even the *agreed* takeover or merger can be fraught with problems. However, whether attacking or defending the risk can be minimized by careful preparation and detailed planning.

Preparing to make a takeover bid

In September 1981 Alexander & Alexander, an established and reputable firm of American insurance brokers announced the purchase of the London-based Lloyd's brokers, Alexander Howden. They paid £150 million in cash and shares for this bridgehead in the London insurance market, which had direct access to the important Lloyd's syndicates. About a year later Alexander & Alexander became concerned and appointed the accountants Deloitte Haskins & Sells to look at the accounts at Alexander Howden. They discovered that many millions of pounds, which should have belonged to Alexander & Alexander, had gone missing. The story has now become part of the history of Lloyd's scandals. Alexander & Alexander found themselves burdened with lawsuits, investigations and damaging rumours to add to their financial losses.

More recently, in May 1986, the Hollywood film group

Cannon acquired ABC Cinemas and Elstree Studios. Within three weeks of the purchase Cannon complained of poorly negotiated contracts and gross incompetence.

It is difficult to see how Alexander & Alexander could have spotted the problems in Alexander Howden prior to the takeover, because certain of the activities were highly irregular and well hidden. The risk was there and in this instance Alexander & Alexander lost. In the case of the Cannon purchase there was reason to be cautious, because the business had changed hands only three weeks before. Cannon paid £50 million more than the previous purchaser, Alan Bond. To pay this much more and then to find that all was not well suggests that the risks of the purchase were not assessed as carefully as they should have been.

How can would-be purchasers reduce such risks? The first step is to determine what attributes of the target company are being sought. This might include, for example:

- Technical expertise or patent rights
- A foothold in a market
- Undervalued assets
- A particular product
- Economies resulting from amalgamation
- Greater market dominance

Knowing precisely *why* the other company is wanted concentrates attention on the aspects of it which particularly require careful investigation. There will, in addition, be other questions to be answered in the assessment which will help to reduce risk.

1 Financial aspects

- Is detailed accounting information available for the past five years and what picture does it present?
- What are the estimates for future profits and cash flow and how will the takeover/merger affect them?
- What is the value of the company assets and the value of any that become surplus as a result of the takeover?

2 Products and markets

- What are the company's products and what are the sales volumes in the various markets?
- What is the reputation of these products and the services provided with them?
- What are the expected future trends in the market involved? Is there a reasonable prospect of growth or is this perhaps a market to be adversely affected in some way?
- Will the takeover extend the market or market share?

3 Equipment

- How up-to-date is the target company's equipment and machinery?
- Is their equipment compatible with your own — to what extent is this important?

4 Development

- What is the quality of the target company's research and development work?
- Will the takeover result in opportunities to share research and development costs?

5 Personnel

- Will redundancies be involved? What is the likely cost? What will be the reaction of the unions and the public?
- What about the company's senior people? Will they be an asset? What is their reputation?
- What administrative problems can arise, *e.g.* differences in wage scales, pension benefits, holidays?

6 Costs

- What form will payment take? Cash, shares, both?
- What is the highest price you are prepared to pay?
- What will be the costs of preparing for and carrying out

the takeover? *e.g.* publicity and legal fees. The degree of resistance expected must be estimated when working out the costs.

- What costs are likely to arise *after* the takeover? *e.g.* in reorganizing office systems, retaining staff, publicity and public relations, rationalizing production, reorganizing marketing and distribution etc.

Great care must be taken with the calculation of revenues and costs. While takeovers can be an effective way to expand a business they can also be an effective way to go bankrupt. The difficulty usually lies in striking a sensible balance between acquisition costs and subsequent revenue, especially when the way of presenting the figures depends on the accounting method used. Some accountants favour a traditional form of acquisition accounting whilst others favour the more recently introduced convention, merger accounting. Neither method is perfect and the whole picture is further clouded by the way in which companies report their profits. Technical adjustments and asset revaluations can substantially change the picture to suit the wishes of the company.

A final consideration is the possibility that there will be problems with the Monopolies Commission or Office of Fair Trading.

The above questions may not take account of every aspect to be considered in any individual case but working carefully through them will mean that the bulk of the homework is done. In addition background information on how many top people have left the target company, and for what reasons, in recent years can give an indication of the state of morale and the quality of those people who remain.

The follow-up

Successfully completing a takeover marks the end of one activity but the beginning of another. Having overcome the risk of failure to make the bid the victorious company must tackle the risk in managing the new, larger operation to a level of profit. There are two approaches to the follow-up: 'hands-off' and 'hands-on'.

The 'hands-off' method

This is the approach practised by Hanson Trust. Hanson leaves the various parts of their empire to get on with managing their own affairs and limits control to tight financial management. This is, of course, a very powerful control but it does not prevent divisional management from changing old products or developing new ones. Research can be done, staff taken on and virtually any local decisions taken *providing* budget constraints are adhered to.

The use of this method means that any target company must have a good middle management which can be relied upon to do the job. There is, however, the risk that such managements will not readily accept corporate control of finance, with the result that some or all of the really entrepreneurial people will depart.

The 'hands-on' method

Using this method means that less attention need be paid to the quality of the target company's management as the company carrying out the takeover does so with every intention of moving in to run it. Examples can be found in the hotel and catering industry, where the victorious company will usually place its own managers in key positions, and impose its own standard on such details as menus, bedmaking and guest registration forms.

Those practising or intending to practise the hands-on method will require confidence in their abilities and a good post-acquisition management team. They must be prepared to face substantial opposition from existing management and staff who will at least be worried by events and in many cases will be actively rebellious. Money may need to be spent in paying off senior people. A comprehensive management package must be imposed, which will require skilled people to install and operate it and to deal with overt or covert resistance, and retraining.

Despite the difficulties in this approach many managements prefer it and take the view that even a prolonged hiccup in the fortunes of the acquired business is better than allowing the old regime to continue. This is obviously the case when the target company was identified as one which was badly managed but offered potential. In such cases the sooner the new regime is imposed the better.

The defence to a takeover

The risk of losing a takeover battle is greatly reduced if the target company is well prepared for the battle. Often a company, finding itself the target for a takeover, will lose valuable time putting its defence together. The time lost can be critical and can result in expensive action being taken under great pressure.

It should be part of the policy of any company likely to be attractive to a predator to have a battle plan continuously ready for action. This plan will incorporate details of the range of defensive actions likely to be necessary, and will specify a defence team who should be ready and able to swing into action at short notice.

The following is a check-list of the defensive actions likely to be necessary:

1   Fast and accurate evaluation of the bid and a realistic comparison with company assets, performance and prospects. In other words is the bid in the interests of the shareholders? Naturally, if the bid is shown to be in the interests of the shareholders, the board will accept the offer and no further defensive action will be required. It is of course quite unethical for management to fight the bid merely to preserve their own personal positions.

2   Approaches to the Office of Fair Trading.

3   Approaches to the Monopolies Commission.

4   Provision of information to institutional and individual shareholders.

5   Clear and prompt explanations to employees with reassurances that their interests and future will not be neglected.

6   Information to financiers, lessors, landlords and suppliers.

7	Information to tenants and customers.
8	Prompt and convincing statements to the media.
9	Advertising and publicity designed to win the support of individual shareholders and the general public.
10	Production of a range of accurate and convincing financial projections, reports, analyses and fact sheets.
11	Contact friendly politicians.

To carry out these activities a defence team should be appointed in advance. They should be kept up-to-date with any relevant information such as changing political attitudes, experience of other companies and trade union thinking. In addition, the company will need the help of specialist outsiders such as advertising and public relations consultants, lawyers, bankers, stock brokers etc. Such experts should also be selected in advance and their competence reviewed from time to time.

The defence team should be ready to act following a bid by bringing the various experts into play — without delay — and by working through the checklist of actions to be carried out. Much time can be saved by having all the details sorted out in advance such as the names and telephone numbers of all individuals who should be kept informed, and access to fast, reliable, high quality printing, binding and mailing services.

Ideally the defence team will meet regularly, say, every three months to consider the likelihood of a bid, review and revise the battle plan and confirm company policy in respect to a bid.

The value of preparations of this sort is well illustrated by the comments made by the management of Allied-Lyons when reviewing the 1985 bid for its company by Elders IXL. Tony Pratt, a member of the defence team was reported (*Financial Times* 27th September, 1986) as saying that the earlier days of the battle were 'hard going'. Members of the defence team were brought in from the divisions with no experience of defence strategy and with little knowledge of each other. The chairman pointed out that the company did not know instinctively how to handle the situation and that reaction to events was on a day-to-day basis. Allied-Lyons management also referred to the importance of a centrally organized communications network.

A further element in fighting off an unwelcome bid is cost. When Aitken Hume, the financial services group fought off a bid from Tranwood Group the defence costs amounted to almost one million pounds resulting in them passing a dividend in 1986. Consideration must be given to ways and means to finance a defence. Some contingency plans prepared in advance may ease the problem and, for instance, reduce borrowing costs which can arise when time is too short to seek other options.

The poison pill

An anti-takeover device which has become prominent since the start of the 1970s is the so-called poison pill. The objective is to make a takeover prohibitively expensive. The procedure is to arrange that when a purchase has taken place shareholders acquire rights to buy additional stock at a heavily discounted rate. There are widely differing views as to whether or not such devices are fair, but they have proved highly effective in the USA. It has been reported that as many as a quarter of the top 500 US companies have adopted the poison pill as a defensive measure.

2

Recruiting a key person

There are a number of situations in which a business will
seek a recruit from the outside world for a key position.
Someone with exceptional skills may be needed to lead a team
managing a promising innovation or to inject sophisticated
financial control into a business with cash flow difficulties. A
strong leader may be required with experience of reviving an
ailing business, or a scientist to carry out research in a pioneer
field. The possibilities are many and all of them present a
clear risk — that of recruiting the wrong person. The risk is
not limited to finding that the skills and expertise of the
newcomer are not up to the standard required to do the job
but can also include the antagonism and disruption caused
by a wholly incompatible personality. A rough, tough whizz-
kid may not go down well in a quiet and perhaps old-
fashioned environment and the academic, professorial personality may not succeed in a demanding rat race.

The damage which can result from recruiting the wrong
person can be so great that it must be regarded as a major
risk. There are some cases, of course, where it will be a
deliberate choice to bring in someone who is not compatible
with the culture of the business, for example where a company
has become mediocre and needs shaking up. The choice of
the person to do the job is still fraught with risk since he or
she may turn out not to be tough enough when trouble starts
or alternatively, may go too far, too fast and wreck the busi-

ness. The effect on British Leyland if someone of less ability than Michael Edwardes had been chosen to sort out its troubles can be imagined.

Regrettably there is no perfect solution to the problem of selecting the right person but the risk can be reduced by a conscious realization of the attributes to be sought and a knowledge of the strengths and weaknesses of the main selection methods. Almost any structured method of selection will be better than taking on the chairman's brother-in-law or the impressive-sounding character that the MD met over lunch at the CBI conference. Nor is it good enough to choose someone solely because he formerly held a prestige job elsewhere. One of the characteristics of British industry is the appearance of certain people in key jobs in which they last about twelve months, receive a large golden handshake and pop up again in another prestige position. Eventually they disappear, but will have left a trail of destruction behind them.

The three main attributes

A successful recruit will satisfy three requirements — compatibility, commitment and competence.

Compatibility is normally the most difficult to assess, since it depends, not only on the individual but on his or her potential colleagues. Every organization has its own culture, from the fast-moving world of the consumer goods market to the more ponderous and gentlemanly environment of a law firm. It is not easy to identify the culture of one's own organization, nor to assess how another person will fit into it.

Commitment is a little easier to measure and normal interviewing techniques can generally be relied upon. The answers given to appropriate questions (e.g. 'Why do you want to work for us?') will normally suffice.

Competence, at least in a technical sense, is the easiest attribute to measure. Professional qualifications will be a good indication and when combined with track record can give a good overall guide to likely performance. The aeronautical designer who has already produced four successful light aircraft is likely to be able successfully to design a fifth one

178

(everything else being equal). A financial expert who has succeeded in turning round a company almost certainly knows how to do it again.

However easy or difficult the assessment of the person may be the method or methods used for selection are of prime importance in reducing the risk. There are three main categories:

- Using a professional head-hunter
- Using personal contact
- Advertising

Each method should be preceded by a *thorough* examination of what it is the recruit will be asked to do and what type of person is required. A clear job description is needed and a profile of the ideal person, because the chance of recruiting the wrong person is inevitably high if there is any doubt as to what he is expected to achieve.

If a competent head-hunter is used he will insist on a job description, and work with you on writing it. He will also draw up a profile of the ideal person. The other methods do not impose this discipline. The pros and cons of each method are compared in the following tables.

	Pros	*Cons*
Head-hunter	1 A good head-hunter will have specialists able to identify his client's particular needs.	1 Poor quality head-hunters exist who merely keep a register of people looking for a job.
	2 The identity of the client can be concealed from the world at large.	2 The field of search is limited to a small population and the best people may be overlooked.
	3 The head-hunter can provide selection skills.	3 High cost.

179

Using a head-hunter may sometimes be the only way to 'catch the eye' of a particular person or persons if there is a reluctance to 'go public' with an advertisement. The high cost of using a head-hunter (not less than 20% of the agreed salary, plus expenses) should be considered in the light of the potential cost resulting from employing the wrong person.

	Pros	*Cons*
Personal contact	1 Providing that the person having the contact is capable of making a good judgement, compatibility problems are dealt with.	1 If anything goes wrong serious embarrassment can be caused.
	2 Low cost.	2 The method is subject to the preferences and prejudices of one individual.

The usual result of using the personal contact method is to find someone who is compatible but similar to the people already in the company. The method tends to discourage the recruitment of people who will introduce new ideas and attitudes into the business.

	Pros	*Cons*
Advertising	1 The job is publicized to the widest possible audience.	1 In-house expertise is needed to sort out the applicants.
	2 People who would not otherwise think	2 The advertisement must be carefully

about changing jobs are prompted to do so.	written to comply with company image.
3 Cost effective — if successful.	3 The best person for the job may not see the advertisement.
4 Can be a source of people for other vacancies.	
5 By producing a variety of applicants can result in a useful change of mind as to what kind of person is wanted.	

A good advertisement, carefully and skilfully worded can sell the company as well as the job.

The use of a structured method for selecting a key employee (or for that matter any employee) is not practised by every company. A survey of companies reported in the November 1986 issue of the British journal *Personnel Management* showed that about 20% of the companies studied failed to conduct interviews in all cases (1% never used interviews at all) and about a third did not bother with references in all cases. About 4% *never* took up references. These companies may have had other methods of assessing applicants which make interviews and references unnecessary but it is difficult to see what these methods could be.

The risk in taking on the wrong person is high because the damage can be considerable. The salary costs alone should be enough to encourage care to be taken — costs which can be measured in millions of pounds. An executive earning an average of £50,000 per year over ten years will cost his company £500,000, after all, and the basic salary is by no means all that needs to be considered. One personnel director was reported to have calculated that in 30 years a

£20,000-a-year employee actually costs his employers £2,250,000.

The follow-through

Companies who have successfully recruited the right person for the job have dealt with one form of risk but now face another. The new person, however good, can rarely be expected to work entirely alone, without willing support from his colleagues. Fear, jealousy and disappointment can all cause existing members of staff to distrust a newcomer — even to the point where the newcomer is rendered entirely ineffective. One technique for doing this is to agree with everything he says but then to do nothing. The possibility of an unhelpful and unfriendly response to the newcomer should be kept in mind when selecting him, something covered of course, by the question of compatibility. It can be argued that the selected person should have shown sufficient strength of personality to deal with antagonism. Even a compatible and capable recruit should be supported by a planned induction programme.

Such a programme will start before the newcomer arrives. His role should be explained to the staff and, where appropriate, reassurance should be given. A useful measure is to arrange for the recruit to meet his future colleagues in an informal and friendly atmosphere, before he starts. A meeting over an unhurried lunch, for instance, provides an opportunity for the newcomer and his future colleagues to become acquainted.

After arrival a key employee should be given time to develop a feel for the business. He should not normally be pressured into making sweeping changes by the end of his first week — such activities are likely to be based on an inadequate appreciation of the situation and can result in serious errors. In one particular case, a key recruit was asked to recommend organizational changes and to state what should be done to improve the company administration on his *third day!* Such rapid activities should be limited to the most serious situations where drastic action is unavoidable.

Time should be allowed for a newcomer to visit factories and other work places, to talk with employees at all levels, customers, suppliers and so on. Management should assist him by making themselves available for discussion and explanation. It should be remembered that a newcomer will have little or no detailed knowledge of past events, like the influences of individuals on decisions which have been taken, and who the really influential people are now.

Any action which is taken to ease the arrival of a newcomer into the management structure will serve to reduce the risk inherent in this type of innovation.

The quality problem

A potential decline in the quality of a product or a service is one of the continuous risks facing a business. The problem can be subtle: the deterioration can be so gradual as to be virtually imperceptible, it causes customer complaints and, ultimately, loss of business. The risk is made worse by the fact that once a reputation for poor quality is established it can be very difficult to dislodge. It is sometimes said that it takes five times as long to rebuild a reputation as it took to lose it.

Most manufacturing businesses will endeavour to control quality using well-established sampling and statistical techniques. More subjective methods are sometimes used in the service industries, like telephoning their own offices to see how they are treated, or, say, in the hotel and catering industry, sending someone to try a meal in the restaurant.

There is nothing wrong with using such methods, all of them being a serious attempt to reduce risk. There is, however, a weakness in the thinking behind these tests of quality in that a percentage failure rate is expected. This is not quite the same as accepting that absolute perfection is not a realistic target. Consider for example the quality standards of British Rail.

In a publication called *Leisure Express*, given away to customers in the summer of 1986, British Rail said, 'It is estimated that punctuality has reached *the target figure of 90 per cent* right time or within five minutes'. This is another way of saying that British Rail *expects* to let down their customers 10% of the time, and is not even thinking about trains being precisely on time as being a necessary target at all.

What would be the reaction of the customers of a bank if, for instance, it claimed to get 90% of its transactions right — within a few pounds of the exact figure?

On the face of it British Rail has a built-in failure rate. Commercial organizations facing competition cannot afford this situation. They would do well to consider adopting the zero defect attitude.

The zero defect attitude

This attitude is that the only *acceptable* failure rate is zero.

Any attitude to quality which is less demanding is an invitation to make mistakes. Such an attitude would not be acceptable in a payroll department or in a parachute packing team so why should it be acceptable anywhere else?

One of the reasons why certain Japanese products have eliminated their former western competition is that the zero defect attitude has been adopted by them both in product quality and in service. This is not to say that the Japanese never get it wrong but that they expect to get it right and they make sure that their workers adopt the same approach.

Quality is another area where the responsibility for the level of risk accepted rests firmly with management. Adopting the zero defect attitude is, after all, only going along with what the customer expects.

4

Trading in foreign markets

There are two major areas of risk in trading in foreign markets: political risk and financial risk. They are closely linked and any attempt at risk assessment must include both types simultaneously.

There is no scientific method for assessing these risks. Management must rely heavily on common sense and judgment. There are however warning signs which can be spotted and a methodical examination of the attributes of a country and its business and political style can at least provide guidance. It must be accepted however that no amount of enquiry can reliably forecast every catastrophic event which may occur — a fact which will be painfully obvious to companies trading with Argentina prior to the Falklands conflict. Neither is it easy to forecast the equally damaging but less dramatic changes, like the gradual deterioration of Brazil from an economic miracle to an economic nightmare.

What can a company do to predict these sorts of risk? The first rule is to examine the country *as a whole* and not just the company or companies with whom trading is contemplated. It may be in slow economic decline: however good the customer's credit rating they may be prevented by national circumstances from meeting their obligations in the future. The following points should be considered:

1   The ease with which the country can generate foreign exchange, and its availability to the companies with whom you wish to trade. If you are being paid in an obscure, and possibly declining, currency, the cost could be high.

2   The political attitude to foreign debts. Is there a chance that under pressure foreign debts will be ignored? Will your customers be prevented by regulations from sending money to you?

3   A markedly high cost of living. This could indicate an overvalued exchange rate, which in turn could suddenly collapse.

4   A high inflation rate.

5   Evidence of social instability — riots, oppressive policing and kangaroo courts. These may lead to a *coup d'état*, with sharp changes in attitude from the new regime. Your customers may even disappear following a military takeover if their companies are politically unacceptable.

6   Corruption. Some companies have made the mistake of believing that they can exploit the system by joining in the '10% for the Minister' game. Things may go well for a time until someone else pays 15% or the minister winds up dead or in jail. If corruption is the norm then the normal rules of business will not apply and there will be no stability in the trading environment.

Unfortunately there are no formal techniques which will help in identifying these factors or measuring their importance. Mathematical models have been constructed by academics to demonstrate the stability or otherwise of national political systems but these have not proved to be of any real practical value.

Judgement must be based on a wide range of contacts including local agents, the foreign office and other government departments, or the experience of others trading in the country concerned. A visit should be made to the country before any trading is agreed if there is any doubt that things will go well. There may of course be preventative measures which can be taken, such as insisting on hard currency deposits in a bank outside the country.

For companies already established in a foreign market the process of looking to the future and assessing the political and other dangers must be a continuous process. Paterson Zochonis, long established in Nigeria, were forced, in 1986, to write off £35 million of assets in that country. Nigeria, after a series of *coups d'état* and successive military governments, devalued its currency by 30%. Some 70% of Paterson Zochonis' group profits normally derived from its activities in Nigeria, but they fell in 1985–86 by 50% with an even lower figure forecast for 1986–87. Stock market expectations included a sharp drop in future profits as a result of the Nigerian experience. If the company had been dependent on Nigerian business alone the situation might have been calamitous.

Investment opportunities

People with ideas for new businesses seek investors. If only small sums are being sought the risk to the investor will be small but where large sums are required the risk can be substantial. Assessing a venture can be difficult, and a methodical approach to measuring the risk and making a decision is necessary.

In the late 1960s and early 1970s a variety of pyramid selling schemes tempted large numbers of small investors to invest their savings in get-rich-quick offers. Any calm and logical examination of these schemes would have established that they were bound to come to grief.

What should a serious businessman do when presented with an investment opportunity? Assuming that the idea is not rejected immediately, a series of test questions can be applied:

1   Is the business already well established or does the offer involve setting up an entirely new concern? Obviously an investment opportunity in an existing business is more attractive because the owners of the business have something to lose, and the track record of the business and its managers can be examined. An entirely new business may well turn out to be a winner but will have no track record.

2   What is the size of the investment asked for? Although a small investment represents a small risk it should be borne in mind that the time, trouble and cost of properly monitoring the investment will be the same as for a large investment. It is not unknown for investors of small amounts to take only a limited interest in how their money is being used, but the less the attention paid to it the more the investment becomes a gamble rather than a considered risk.

3   What is the experience of the managers in the market concerned? Wide experience in one market does not mean that the managers will be successful in another.

4   What technological skills are required to manage the business? Care must be taken to ensure that if the venture is highly technical provision of the essential expertise is not dependent on one man.

5   What is the quality of the management team?

6   If there is a shortage of any particular management skill will the company accept an additional board member to provide it? Any unwillingness to accept professional help in the form of an additional director or perhaps a less senior specialist should be treated with caution.

7   Is there a good, convincing business plan? If there is no business plan including cash flow forecasts, sales estimates and budgets, the risk of failure will be high. Lack of a plan means either that no homework has been done or that the scheme is a potential confidence trick.

Any plan presented should be subjected to a rigorous examination which challenges all the assumptions made about market size, market share, costs, competition and so on. There will almost inevitably be divergence of opinion on some of the elements of the plan, but in the event that there is a *significant* difference of opinion it is helpful either to work out your own plan (using your own estimates) or ask an independent person to do it.

Coping with a crisis

A crisis can hit a business at any time. It could range from the kidnapping of the chairman to a product liability problem.

The Union Carbide disaster in Bhopal is a clear example of the possible extent of a major crisis. The results of the Bhopal incident included:

- Thousands of victims and great suffering
- Censure in the press
- Attacks from politicians
- A sharp drop in share price
- Substantial loss of assets
- Financial losses and increased expenditure

It should not be imagined that such problems will arise only from dramatic incidents of the Bhopal type. A drug found to have serious side effects or an attempt to poison the products of a food company could be equally damaging. Nor is a crisis necessarily limited in location and time. The loss of the *Kowloon Bridge* off the Irish coast in November 1986, following the unexplained loss of a sister ship in 1980, raised queries about the safety of other sister ships and led to calls from the Hong Kong Merchant Navy Officers Guild for a government enquiry.

The discovery that asbestos, widely used for many years,

can cause lung disease has resulted in many hundreds of health claims and substantial problems for many businesses. Since there is a delayed reaction to exposure to asbestos the crisis is, for victims and businesses alike, spread over many years.

The important question for the managers of a business is how to prepare for a potential crisis. Once it has occurred losses will be inevitable, but they can be contained most effectively by having carefully prepared contingency plans available. The following are the minimum steps which a business can take to avoid further risk in the aftermath of a crisis:

What could happen to our business?

Some types of crisis are more likely in some businesses than in others. A bank, for example, could face a massive fraud but is not likely to be implicated in a pollution scandal. Listing, in descending order of likelihood, the threats which the business faces will help to focus thinking on the problem. Examples to consider include product liability, terrorism, natural disaster, hostile takeover bids, pollution, fraudulent action by employees, strikes or even a purely financial crisis.

How good are our preventative measures?

A regular review of risk-reducing measures has been recommended already in this book, but it is particularly important when planning for dealing with a crisis. It is always possible that having completed the identification of potential disasters that something new in the way of a threat has been spotted. In each case it is important to analyse as carefully as possible the implications of a potential crisis, and the likely effectiveness of existing defences.

What is the policy?

There is nothing worse in the middle of a crisis than a board-room argument over policy. Time-wasting and potentially divisive arguments over attitudes to publicity, the public, employees and government agencies can seriously aggravate a crisis. A fast response is needed to a crisis, not only in terms of physical precautions but also in communication with the world at large.

Whoever leads the response should be able to do so in the knowledge that there will be full and consistent backing from colleagues. Disagreement or conflict can damage the company image and reduce the effectiveness of defence measures. Similarly, a policy decision is needed on any costly action which may be needed. When Johnson & Johnson, the US manufacturers of the painkiller Tylenol found itself in 1982 with capsules in the shops which had been laced with poison they decided to withdraw the product from the market. This cost them about $100 million, an expensive decision which was taken even though poisoned Tylenol was found only in one place. The result was widespread public approval. The company was perceived as a responsible, caring one. Had Johnson & Johnson spent weeks or months agonizing over the cost before making a decision the result could have been very different. As it was, its response brought public approbation to the extent that Tylenol, marketed in new, tamper-proof bottles, captured an even greater market share than it had enjoyed before the crisis.

Who does what?

The most important step, having identified as far as possible the main types of crisis which could occur and the company policy to be followed, is to create a crisis management team with a plan of action.

The team must comprise senior people with wide authority, including a team leader and technical, communications and financial experts. The exact make-up of the team will depend on the nature of the business and the type of crisis. These are some of the tasks it will have to perform:

1   Coordination of action taken and reporting back to the board of directors. Often the chief executive has been

expected to coordinate the response to a crisis. This can place too great a burden on someone who will have all his other duties to perform and will be in demand by politicians, government agencies, consumers and the media. The burden of practical action should be placed on the team which should have no other function than to handle the crisis.

2   Assessing all the facts and implications. In a major crisis there is often a good deal of confusion. Hard facts tend to be disguised by rumour and speculation. Obtaining the real facts often means placing specialists on the site who can make professional judgments as to the true state of affairs. Only when the full picture is accurately assessed can its personnel, publicity, marketing and legal implications be determined.

3   Damage limitation. Deciding what must be done and getting it started will be an important requirement not only to contain the loss but to reassure everyone concerned that action is being taken. The policy towards expenditure is crucial and it is an absolute necessity that the team know how far they can go. Any delay while financial approval is being obtained can worsen the crisis and provoke criticism from the press and public.

4   Communicating with outsiders. Effective communication with the media, the public, consumers and suppliers is the key to good crisis management. A positive stance must be adopted. A refusal to give information to the media will cause them to either speculate or to seek it elsewhere. Either reaction can be very damaging — it is clearly better for a company spokesman to answer questions than for an outside and possibly hostile expert to be asked to comment.

Effective, and if appropriate sympathetic, communication will be required with those affected by the crisis. The emphasis must be on assuring them that the company is acting quickly, positively and responsibly.

Some crises, or their aftermath, will drag on for a long

time. Allowances should be made for the stress and fatigue which can result and which is often more marked in the later stages when the initial excitement has died down and the job has become more routine. The crisis management team should be large enough to allow its members to take rest breaks from time to time.

A crisis efficiently dealt with can mean survival, or even an opportunity, for a company. Not being prepared presents a risk of going under.

Using intrapreneurial skill

There is a slow but positive change of attitude in many businesses to the 'intrapreneur'. This is an employee who has an idea for an innovation and who wants to develop it. He is, in effect, an internal entrepreneur, who contributes enthusiasm and enterprise of a 'small business' type within a larger company framework. Too often in the past the notion that a junior employee can come up with a really worthwhile commercial proposition has been treated with scorn. Following some examples of intrapreneurial success, however, and with the support of enthusiasts here and there, a greater willingness is developing to exploit the bright ideas of those within the business at whatever level. It is becoming recognized that a company with 1,000 employees has 1,000 brains available to it and that at least some of these brains will have potentially winning ideas from time to time.

There remains, however, the problem of controlling the intrapreneur. There is an understandable reluctance to allow intrapreneurs to expend time and money developing pet schemes, which may come to nothing. How can a company reduce the risk of wasted time and money but at the same time avoid throwing away potentially profitable opportunities?

The answer is, first, having assessed the idea with an open mind, to give the intrapreneur a limited freedom to act.

A tight but realistic budget can be provided for the first stage of the project with the clear understanding that going on to a further stage will be dependent on satisfactory results. This gives the intrapreneur the opportunity to develop the idea but limits the risk to the business.

Secondly, appoint a senior person to act as 'Godfather' to keep an eye on what is happening and to help the intrapreneur. The Godfather can provide advice and also smooth the path for the intrapreneur who may have opposition from those to whom he goes for resources or information.

These measures will reduce the risk but ensure that ideas are not consigned to the scrap heap without being given a chance. There is always the other risk that failure to support an intrapreneur will cause him to leave, taking his idea to a competitor who will profit from it.

Credit and cash flow

All businesses face an actual or a potential cash flow problem from time to time. In serious cases a developing cash flow crisis can bring the business to its knees, as funds become inadequate to pay wages, buy raw materials or to meet other essential expenses. One of the major causes of cash problems is delay in collecting money due from debtors. Many companies concentrate a lot of effort on credit control and obtaining credit ratings via companies specializing in this service. This is perhaps the first line of defence in reducing the risk of bad debts but it does little to reduce the risk of damaging overdue debts, which can be just as serious. Positive measures are needed to contain the problem, which must take account of the way in which modern businesses deal with invoices sent to them.

How are invoices dealt with?

Increasingly businesses operate their purchase ledger on a computer. This normally means that a payment run is made once a month. If this is carried out on say, the 25th of the month, then any invoice arriving on the 26th will have to wait at least a month before it receives attention. To this delay must be added the time taken to prepare a cheque (if not part of the computer run) and the time which elapses before the accountant gets round to signing it. In all probability a second signatory will be required and yet more time will elapse before this person attends to the cheque. If mailing time is added it is likely that about six weeks will elapse from the time the invoice arrives to the time that the payment is despatched. In addition the invoice may relate to expenditure made on raw materials and labour some weeks before it was sent to the customer so that the total elapsed time from spending money to getting it back can easily be two months.

If, in the meantime, the invoice has been found to contain a real or imagined error it could be put aside by the recipient until the error is referred back to the sender for clarification — which takes up still further time.

The average delay for the payment of invoices can amount to about sixty days and this represents a sizeable loss of revenue. A million pounds invested at say 8% per annum for sixty days would yield about £13,300. This is the annual cost of the credit given to customers if there is a million pounds on average outstanding throughout the year. If profits amount to say, a net 3% on sales then the lost investment earnings of £13,300 are equivalent to about £443,000 of lost sales. However, these costs are the tip of the iceberg and the real risk is the one of having insufficient liquidity to continue to operate the business.

The solution to the problem of how to reduce the risk once again lies in the hands of management, which can install a number of simple precautions in the sales accounting procedures.

The sales accounting procedures

The first step is to ensure that *all* invoices are despatched *promptly* (*e.g.* within 48 hours) of the order being completed. This not only reduces the contribution to the delay made by the invoicing company itself but also reduces the chance of missing the customer's monthly payments run. One company, which sent all its invoices to a major customer in monthly batches (with a statement), had frequent battles with the customer over payment delays. It eventually realized that its own monthly run resulted in its invoices just missing the customer's monthly run which took place about two working days later. It then switched to daily invoicing and collected its money more quickly.

The next step is to build in a checking system to see that invoices are correct. This check should cover mathematical accuracy *and* the manner in which the invoice is prepared. If the goods or service are badly or incorrectly described an opportunity for delay is created. Also, some companies ask for invoices to be prepared in particular ways or with extra copies and these requirements should also be met.

Another company with payment problems found, after many months of complaining, that the cause of the delay was that they sent their invoices to the address of the customer's factory — not to the head office from which payments were made, and to which they had been asked to send their invoices. The recipient at the factory made no urgent effort to redirect the invoices received and two or three weeks were lost each time.

Another aspect worth watching is the size of the amount invoiced. In many companies the higher the amount to be paid the higher the payment must go in the management hierarchy for approval. This often means delay, especially if the amount is so large that the chief executive is involved. Such people tend to be busy and are often absent on business trips, resulting in further hold-ups until the debt can be attended to.

For this reason it is rarely worth accumulating charges and putting a number of them on one invoice. Although this is often done to save clerical work it also has the effect of raising the total to be paid and creating more bureaucratic delay in the customer's office.

The terms of sale

Another area worthy of management attention is the terms of sale negotiated with customers in the first place. Cases occur where no negotiation takes place at all and the supplying company relies on terms and conditions provided in small print on the back of the invoice. If these terms are noticed at all they are probably noticed too late or are ignored.

Part of the sales function should be to arrange and agree payment terms in advance. There is then at least a chance of reasonable payment periods being achieved.

Giving it to the professionals

Factoring is a method which can save money and, in particular, cut the risk of a cash flow disaster. Factoring companies, in addition to providing invoicing and sales ledger services will advance up to 80% of the invoice value,, thus ensuring that working funds are available. Naturally the factoring companies must be paid a fee for their work but it is unlikely to be uneconomic to use them, especially if money can be saved on sales ledger clerical costs. Above all there is a guarantee of some money coming in promptly and the remainder in reasonable time.

The following questions should be asked in relation to sales ledger efficiency:

1   What percentage of working capital is represented by outstanding debts?
2   What percentage of the amount is over 30 days outstanding?
3   How much is the company paying for bank overdrafts or short-term loans?
4   Does the sales force know of, and work to, a clear credit policy?
5   What is the average delay between completing a delivery or service and despatch of the invoice?
6   What percentage of invoices are queried and for what reason?
7   How soon after the month end are monthly statements sent out?
8   If payment delays could be reduced by say, 25%, what would be the effect on cash flow?

An unsatisfactory answer to any of the first seven of these

questions suggests that there is an opportunity to improve the profits of the business and the answer to the eighth question will indicate by how much profits can be improved.

An unsatisfactory answer to any of the first seven questions also indicates that the cash flow risk can be reduced.

Purchasing policy

In 1980 the British Institute of Management published a report entitled 'The Purchasing Function', based on a study of the purchasing activities of 208 British companies. The report showed that a majority of these businesses (65%) perceived one of their main objectives as being 'to meet the needs of production at economic prices'. The second most popular objective (43% of companies) was 'continuity of supply'. This perhaps sums up the most frequently applied purchasing philosophy, that of dependable supply at low cost.

Traditionally multiple sourcing is used to achieve this end, and the BIM report showed that 88% of their sample companies had more than one supplier for at least some of their product components. More than half of the companies had multiple sources for over 50% of all the items purchased.

This hitherto unchallenged approach to obtaining low prices and reducing the risk of interruption to supply has recently come under attack — partly as a result of the experience of companies in the USA, where single sourcing has, during the 1980s, become more and more popular, with resultant cost reduction. These savings, have enabled some companies to reduce a different risk — that of losing business to foreign competitors.

A major American manufacturer of office machines was reported to have reduced the number of its suppliers by about

85% over five years. It was claimed that this saved it from intense competition from Japanese suppliers.

This US experience has now been examined by Professor Ivor Morgan of Boston University who put forward some thought provoking ideas at Imede, the management training centre at Lausanne in Switzerland. Professor Morgan's main points, some of which are included in a pamphlet on purchasing published by Imede (PO Box 1059, CH–1001 Lausanne, Switzerland) are as follows:

1   The traditional multi-sourcing method distances the purchaser from the supplier and inhibits the latter's design and creative abilities. Working closely with one supplier results in a better product and enables both parties to plan their activities more successfully.
2   Quality problems are easier to find and resolve when only one supplier is used.
3   Concentrating on one supplier results in economies of scale.

It has been reported (*Financial Times* 24th October, 1986) that Professor Morgan accepts that more research is needed into the effects of the purchasing changes taking place in the US — including the failures as well as successes of single sourcing.

The world is changing, however, and maybe increasing price competition is creating a far greater risk of purchase costs being too high than of supplies being interrupted. If close cooperation with a supplier can result in lower prices *and* measures to ensure supply then the best of all possible worlds will have been achieved.

Fraud

Fraud is one of the most common of the pure risks which a business can face and is a topic regularly in the headlines in the business press. There is a natural tendency for the more highly publicized frauds, involving large sums of money, to cause businessmen to concentrate on the prevention of major single-event losses. While precautions to avoid such major losses are clearly necessary the possibility of attritional losses must not be overlooked. A long series of minor frauds can, in total, amount to a greater loss than the single more dramatic event and is often more difficult to detect.

The risk-reducing measures fall into two categories — prevention and detection. Obviously prevention is the most useful of these measures since detection may not result in recovery of the loss. However, the fact that measures have been taken to improve the chances of detection is, in itself, a preventative measure. The knowledge that the crime could be discovered is a powerful deterrent to the potential fraudster.

The types of fraud which can occur will vary from one business to another but the following are some general categories:

1   Diversion of funds into a private bank account
2   Overcharging a customer in collusion with a customer's employee

3   Fake purchases, payment for which is approved by the fraudster
4   False expense claims
5   Stock frauds, *e.g.* faking issues of spare parts which are in fact stolen
6   Approving payments for services which were not actually received
7   Charging personal expenditure to the company
8   Giving unauthorized discounts to customers
9   Frauds involving share dealing
10   Insurance frauds, *e.g.* fake or inflated claims
11   Cheque frauds, *e.g.* the use of forged signatures
12   Falsification of stock-taking records, *e.g.* recording shrinkage losses
13   Ghost employees

There is another category which looms large in the minds of many people — computer frauds. Although meriting some special attention computer frauds are normally, in essence, no different from all the traditional ways to make some illegal gains. The difference is that the computer has made the criminal's activities less easy to prevent and detect. Transactions are less 'visible' when taking place in a computer system, and cash movements can be much faster. In addition, many managers do not understand computer systems, and often more people have access to the system than in the case of the old manual system.

Notwithstanding these difficulties there are positive and effective measures which can be taken to reduce the risk of computer frauds — many of these measures being the same as, or similar to, those required in the case of non-computer frauds.

Prevention and detection

The first requirement in building the defences against frauds is to identify the likely opportunities for the thief and to quantify the exposure to loss. Some careful thinking about the temptations which the business offers can lead to a realization of the vulnerable areas and thus to appropriate security precautions.

A useful practical exercise is to brainstorm the question, 'If I wanted to defraud the company, how could I do it?' Having spotted the fraud possibilities the same brainstorming team can tackle the question, 'How can I be prevented from perpetrating these frauds?'

Such an exercise will result in answers relevant to the particular business concerned but will probably include some of the following:

1   Segregation of duties so that frauds will require the collusion of two or more people.
2   Insisting that staff in sensitive areas take all their holidays and that these holidays are never less than two weeks in duration. Many frauds have been discovered as a result of the absence of the perpetrator who was able to cover his tracks while present.
3   Appointing non-executive directors to the board.
4   Setting up an internal audit department reporting to an audit committee of the board.
5   Implementing paperwork controls such as dual signatories on cheques, credit notes, stock destruction certificates and the like.
6   Insisting that the external auditors report any actual or suspected fraud to the board of directors.
7   Limiting access to sensitive areas such as the cashier's office, computer department, stores and payroll department. In particular, no computer staff other than operators should be allowed into the computer machine room itself. Programmers and systems analysts must be kept separate from the operating function to prevent the misuse of data or unauthorized processing runs.
8   Keeping all computer disks in a library under lock and key. Issues and return of disks should be recorded by a librarian.

It will be seen that most of these precautions are nothing more than common sense measures which should form part of the normal controls in the business. They are nevertheless often neglected and are sometimes even absent as a result of organizational or other changes which have taken place without a rethink of the security arrangements required. The widespread introduction of personal computers and on-line terminal systems in recent years is a case in point: many such installations lack basic defences to malpractice. The difference from the fraud angle between this type of computer system and the older central machine system is that many more people have computer power available to them. In some offices as many as 50% of the staff have access to a terminal or a personal machine and they are often in a position to use the machines of other people as well. This makes it possible for individuals to 'access' a computer system, extract information from it and manipulate or alter the data stored. This facility can provide the fraudster with a golden opportunity. The answer is to use a combination of passwords and cryptography backed up by common sense precautions such as keeping floppy disks under lock and key.

Passwords

The easiest password to correctly guess is the initials of the authorized user of the machine! A more imaginative and less obvious password will prevent most abuses and is a simple way to limit access to a computer system. Confidential information such as payroll or personnel data should be protected by a password. In situations where several machines are in use in a department added security can be gained by using a different password for each machine. The use of a departmental password, common to all machines, can allow unauthorized entry into systems.

Cryptography

Converting data into a code is a solution to the problem of confidential information being intercepted when being transmitted from one computer to another. The use of computers for data transmission is becoming more and more commonplace, as is the technology required to break into the transmission. Indeed, a simple radio is all that is needed to listen in to the most modern form of data transmission — by satellite. Software packages for encryption are available from specialist suppliers — some of whom can give expert advice on their effective use.

Computing

Most people, when considering computing risks, think first of the computer frauds referred to in the previous section. There are oft-repeated stories of programmers telephoning their former employers from a luxury hotel in Rio de Janeiro telling them how they stole a million pounds — stories which give the impression that fraud is the only risk.

This is far from the truth as the experiences of the London Stock Exchange bear witness. Immediately following the so-called Big Bang of 1986, the exchange authorities were obliged to suspend their computerized market price service (SEAQ) several times. It was at first thought that this was due to an overloading of the system by the hundreds of dealers all operating their terminals at once. Later it was discovered that there was a bug in the system. This fault had not shown up in testing — indeed, it could scarcely have done so because the fault was in that part of the software which controlled overuse. SEAQ failed despite every care being taken in its design and preparation. This illustrates one of the risks facing computer-dependent businesses, that faults in the system may not be revealed by testing but will emerge in a damaging way during real-life operation.

The fact that many senior managers are surprised, puzzled and disappointed by such occurrences shows that too many of them know too little about the computer systems, and their technical staff, on which their businesses depend. This situation presents another area of risk which should be dealt with by ensuring that senior non-technical staff have at least a basic understanding of computers, their characteristics and limitations.

The Stock Exchange experience also underlined four other 'Murphy's Laws' of computing:

i.   The system you install will be inadequate.
ii. Software bugs will emerge.
iii. The system will not be ready on time.
iv. The users will wreck the system.

The last of these laws was demonstrated a few weeks after the start-up of the Stock Exchange system when a market maker entered 'false' figures into the system. Incorrect opening *and* closing prices were entered and after remedial action to correct the errors had been taken the 'wrong button was pressed' and the whole lot went back into the system again. To add to the confusion these incorrect prices were subsequently quoted in many newspapers.

The computer system actually had a 'tripwire facility' to query suspect share prices but for some reason this did not work. All of this trouble was despite some very professional system design and user training.

All of this sounds very gloomy and doom-laden but in fact computing risks can be satisfactorily contained if not entirely eliminated. A survey carried out in 1986 by Data-solve, the computer service subsidiary of Thorn EMI, showed that as many as two thirds of reported computer disasters could have been prevented. Once again, as in many other risk situations, most disasters can be prevented by common sense methods. The following are the most common of the risk situations and the appropriate action required:

1 Power failure

Wherever computer users enter data directly to the computer, the sudden loss of power will lead to a risk situation. For example, the computer system may be incapable of recreating the transactions entered during the elapsed period between taking the previous security copy of the computer files and the moment of breakdown. In such an event the users will have to re-enter all the lost work. If no security copy had been taken of the situation prior to the transactions being made then the whole record could be lost following a power failure.

There are two precautions that may be used. The first consists of using a system that is capable of automatically updating a security copy of data files with all transactions up to the point of failure. This, apart from the time period taken up in carrying out the restore operation, carries little risk provided, of course, that the necessary security features are in position.

The second precaution consists of using an uninterruptable power supply (UPS) connected to the computer so that when a power failure occurs, the UPS will step in immediately without any loss of power. This will give the computer operator the opportunity of closing down the system without any loss of work or data.

Typically, a UPS is based on long-lasting batteries which provide an extension of fifteen to twenty minutes of operating time. This amount of time should be adequate in most cases.

2 Malicious act

A computer operator with a grudge may try to sabotage the installation by deleting essential files. He may also prevent the information being restored by removing or corrupting the security copies. Precautions against this kind of action call for off-site storage of extra security copies, administered in such a way that at least one copy will always be off-site, even allowing for the making of fresh copies. Obviously the transit of the off-site security copies cannot be in the hands of the operators or anyone else who may have access to the computer.

3 Fire

In addition to carbon dioxide extinguishers and other standard precautions, data stored on disk or tape must be duplicated and, as protection against malicious acts, be stored off-site. The off-site storage will itself need some fire precautions such as the use of high grade fireproof safes.

Contingency plans are needed, such as arrangements with a bureau or another user of a similar computer (or even a stand-by machine) to enable work to continue if the computer installation is damaged or destroyed by fire. This precaution also protects against loss of services due to flooding or vandalism of machinery.

4 Poor updating

If a system updates information inaccurately and it is not spotted quickly, summary and other extracted information could be wrong, leading to business decisions based on incorrect information. Regular routine checks such as trial balances should be used plus, whenever possible, checks built into the software to detect and reveal unlikely values.

5 System inadequacies

A common problem is finding, some time after start-up, that the system will not do what it was supposed to do. This can present considerable risk to the computer-dependent business.

Emphasis should be placed on prevention and the following are some *basic* precautions:

1   A full and detailed specification for the system should be prepared, in writing, before any equipment is ordered or program written. This specification must take account of all imaginable situations which can arise, *e.g.* volumes of data to be processed, peak times, future expansion to the system and so on. Naturally, the specification must be absolutely clear about what the system is

intended to produce in the way of reports, summaries and listings, and the exact design of this output. All these details must be agreed with the potential users. The system designers must ensure that the users fully understand what they will get and when. It is too late for a user to complain after the system has been created that he is not getting what he thought he was going to get.

2   Terminology must be agreed all round and such terms as 'summary' or 'report' defined in advance.

3   Any programming contracts drawn up with external system suppliers should include a full copy of the specification and an explanation of the terms used.

4   Full testing must be allowed for using, as far as possible, live data as well as specifically designed test data which will test the system to the full. Any built-in checks to reveal errors must be fully tested by submitting contrived errors to the system and seeing if they are picked up.

5   A safety margin of hardware capacity should be built into the system, to allow for uneven work flow.

6   A stand-by machine or other fall-back facility should be considered — especially when a large number of users are dependent on the system. If a stand-by machine is considered too expensive then some other failure contingency plan must be drawn up, according to the likely damage which will result if users of terminals are denied access to information. In some cases, such as airline booking systems, such an event can be instantly disastrous. In others a period of time without the system being available may be tolerable if say, stand-by listings are provided.

6 Data residue

With the increasing use of small personal machines, many of which operate on highly portable floppy disks, there is a danger of sensitive data being left on the disks and being read by unauthorized persons. The erasing of disk files using the 'delete' or 'erase' commands often only results in the setting of a 'file deleted' indicator in the file directory. The data will remain on the floppy disk and it is a simple matter for an unauthorized person to reset the indicator and read the file.

The problem can be solved by using special 'purge' programs which will overwrite the data to be protected.

7 Emanations

It is possible, indeed easy, with inexpensive and readily available equipment to 'listen in' to someone else's computer. Virtually all computer equipment, but in particular visual display units, printers and data-carrying cables emit radio waves which can be picked up. These can be translated into words on the screen of another computer located nearby. Banks and other financial institutions are at risk. Apart from encryption, which we have already mentioned in the section on fraud, two other forms of protection can be provided:

1   Source suppression — based on careful design of circuitry and layout so that no compromising signals are emitted.
2   Encapsulation — a method which relies on the use of radio-frequency filtering techniques and shielding to keep all emanations within the computer room.

These forms of protection add cost to the computer installation but are probably less expensive than allowing valuable data to become available to unauthorized people.

A burglary took place some years ago involving a break-in at a computer centre. The intruders were highly successful and stole vital data. The intruders were assisted by a number of factors which clearly indicate some of the common weaknesses in protective measures:

1   The security guard admitted the intruders because they were well dressed and carried boxes of tapes! The guard was used to people coming in at odd hours.

215

2   The power to the computer was turned off and the switch was in a locked breaker box. However, the keys to the box were stored in the top drawer of the nearest desk.

3   The computer printer was ready set up with paper and a spare roll was lying nearby.

4   A clearly labelled 'boot deck' of assembly language cards was also conveniently to hand.

5   The disks were stored in locked cabinets which were fixed to the wall. When removed from their fittings the cabinets were found to have no backs and the disks could be easily removed.

6   Each disk was clearly labelled with readily understandable acronyms such as PAYOII for the payroll.

7   Operator documentation (of good quality) was lying on the operator's desk in convenient ring binders.

The intruders were able to run the computer, list some valuable data and walk away. The simple precautions which would have prevented the theft are self-evident.

Further reading

In addition to various books and reports already referred to there are a number of other books which readers may find useful.

A good general treatment of insurance may be found in *An Introduction to Risk Management* by Neil Crockford (Woodhead-Faulkner Ltd). This book deals with risk-reduction measures other than insurance but it is insurance which is covered in the greatest detail. Readers wishing to go further in their research into insurance will find a wide range of material on the bookshelves covering the more specialist areas of reinsurance, claims adjusting and so on.

The problems of the professional practice are dealt with in *Professional Negligence* by Jackson and Powell (Sweet & Maxwell). This book is legally orientated but gives a good resumé of the types of risk which must be considered.

Informed criticism of inappropriate accounting techniques is provided in Robert Kaplan's 'Accounting Lag: The Obsolescence of Cost Accounting Systems' in *The Uneasy Alliance — Managing the Productivity/Technology Dilemma* (Harvard Business School Press).

The specialist area of banking risks is dealt with in *Emerging Risks in International Banking* by P.N. Snowden and also in *UK Banking Supervision* edited by P.M. Gardner.

The first of these two books covers such subjects as credit

markets, loss risk and instability in international lending. The second covers banking crises and risks, self-regulation and risk-related deposit insurance. Dealing with crises is described in *Crisis Management* by Michael Regester (Hutchinson Business).

An interesting survey of credit control and debt collection practices is described in *Management Survey Report No 52*, published by the British Institute of Management. The BIM also offers *Management Survey Report No 50* on purchasing and the following further publications relevant to risk: *Investment Appraisal*, by J.G. Worby; *Introduction to Creative Thinking and Brainstorming*, by J.R. Rawlinson; *Guidelines for Product Innovation, by Dr R.C. Parker; Managing New Product*, by G. Randall.

Help with the problem of recruiting a key person is given in the BIM's two books, *How to Interview* by Mackenzie Davey & McDonnell, and *How to Recruit* by Braithwaite & Schofield.

The difficult area of computing risks is tackled by Peter Hamilton in a now elderly book (1972) *Computer Security* (Associated Business Programmes). The good basic advice given is still relevant although the technology has changed.

Information on computing risks is also included in a more up-to-date work, *Corporate Fraud* by Jack Bologna (Butterworth). Published in 1984, this book includes a chapter on fraud investigation in what is termed 'the electronics data processing era' and a glossary of computer fraud techniques and counter measures.

Finally, a series of hypothetical but realistic problems are posed and answered in *The Best of Dilemma and Decision* published by McGraw-Hill. This book is a compilation of articles which have appeared in the magazine *International Management*. The various dilemmas described may well provide some useful thinking in the boardroom.

Index

221

224

225